The Health and Wellness Ministry in the African American Church

Preventive Health Education

Reverend Edwin H. Hamilton, M.D., D.Min.

Copyright © 2004 by Reverend Edwin H. Hamilton, M.D., D.Min.

The Health and Wellness Ministry in the African American Church by Reverend Edwin H. Hamilton, M.D., D.Min.

Printed in the United States of America

ISBN 1-594674-69-8

All rights reserved solely by the author. The author guarantees all contents are original and do not infringe upon the legal rights of any other person or work. No part of this book may be reproduced in any form without the permission of the author. The views expressed in this book are not necessarily those of the publisher.

Unless otherwise indicated, Bible quotations are taken from the King James Version of the New Scofield Reference Bible. Copyright © 1967 by Oxford University Press, Inc.

www.xulonpress.com

Table of Contents

Epigraph..7
Dedication..9
Preface 11
The Author's Introduction 13
Acknowledgments 19
Letters of Acknowledgment...21
Guest Introduction 23

Chapter One
    The Theoretical Foundation for the Health
    and Wellness Ministry 33
    Questionnaire/Answers 45

Chapter Two
    The Model in Ministry Design 51

Chapter Three
    Planning the Health and Wellness Ministry 55

Chapter Four
    Water...73

Chapter Five
    Planning the Community Health Fair..................................75

Chapter Six
    Summary and Conclusions 83

Chapter Seven
    Course Outlines for the Health and
    Wellness Ministry 87

Chapter Eight
  Two Sermons:
    Sermon One:
      . "Your Body — Temple of the Holy Spirit."
        Its Creation — Cost — and Care..............................110
    Sermon Two:
      "Is There a Doctor in the House?" 121

Delivered at the June 1997 Hampton University Ministers Conference
Glossary 133
Bibliography 135
Health and Wellness Ministry Exhibits 140

EPIGRAPH
To Health!!

Dedication

To My Parents

Rev. Eli Lenard Hamilton who departed this life twenty-eight years ago. He was a man of honor who has inspired me and continues to do so today. He preached for fifty-six years, but he never heard me preach.

Lucille Grier Hamilton, who went to be with the Lord on November 11, 1994, at the ripe old age of ninetyfour years. She was witty, inspiring, quiet with a strong inner resolve and wisdom unmatched in my life. To God Be The Glory!

Preface

This work is written to introduce and establish throughout the African American Church, a program of Preventive Health Education through a Health and Wellness Ministry. The writer hopes that God's people will start on their journey of diminishing the plethora of devastating diseases which plague our Black Communities.

The Model-in-Ministry presented herein should help Health Ministers and laity to understand and duplicate a Health Ministry in the African American Church. The Health Ministers should become empowered and transformed so as to bring about positive health changes in others. Further, it is the fervent hope of this writer that the Health and Wellness Ministry in the African American Church and Preventive Health Education will reach a positive place of prominence in our churches.

Additionally, it is his unyielding expectation that the journey toward "Health Awareness" should end with all of us, "humankind," "taking charge of our health."

The Author's Introduction

This book is written for African Americans of all faiths, religions, persuasions, beliefs and, most importantly, all denominations. It is a non-denominational book to help everyone healthwise, despite where you choose to worship or what you believe in. Remember that diseases transcend all religious boundaries. This is most important to understand in reading this book.

Paul helps us set the tone for the Health and Wellness Ministry by the question he asks in I Corinthians 6:19 KJV. That query is:

"What? Know ye not that your body is the temple of the Holy Spirit who is in you, whom ye have of God, and ye are not your own?"

Initially, I must say that we know that there are many health problems that affect the African American community, uniquely and disproportionately. I can further elucidate that many of us are cognizant of the fact that the multiplicity and severity of the diseases in the African American community are widespread. They originate from diverse bases of socioeconomic, cultural, ethnic, and educational problems. Late stage diagnoses make ineffective, in most cases, the otherwise effectively positive and curative treatment methods existing in early diagnoses.

Preventive medicine; effective health education leading to prevention and early detection, comprise essential elements of a sound program of health education. They should help to diminish the present trend of crippling diseases that plague our communities. Experientially, I can say that we have lost loved ones, relatives, friends and acquaintances who have succumbed to preventable diseases because of late diagnoses. Should we allow this trend of preventable diseases to continue to devastate our communities? That is the important question which we are asked to ponder now.

There are several factors which impact our communities, but the major one is lack of access or lack of equal access to health care. This factor is a mortal hindrance to its potentially positive benefit which should be granted to all citizens in the community. This is truly evident in the African American community! One might say that surely everyone has access to good health care because there are many freestanding hospitals, clinics, rehabilitation centers, trauma centers, medical offices, etc. with excellent physicians. It is unthinkable that any human being exists without access to medical care, the query could be asked, "Do the aforementioned facilities make for access to health care?" This writer would render an inequivocal no to that question. There are several parts to the concept of "lack of access." Let us look at them briefly:

1. Transportation (or the lack thereof) — This part is of the utmost import. The question that clearly becomes known is this: What good is all the modern technology, innovations, the greatest medical facilities in the world, and the best doctors if a person doesn't have transportation to get to them? A possible exception is when 911-EMS is called and it is many times too late! It should be understood that if a patient, any patient, is able to get to the facility and is denied the proper treatment, that still constitutes "lack of access." The lack of transportation access leads to and is interwoven with number two.

2. Economic Depravity — In this society, the cliché "money talks" rings forever true for the African American. It is well documented that poverty levels are higher in our communities. Does it matter that we boast of having the best of the best doctors and "Rolls Royce" hospitals in the world, when many of our citizens don't have bus fare to get to them? By-products of economic depravity are uninsured, underinsured, underserved, unserved, underemployed and unemployed to a disproportionately large degree in the African-American communities.

3. Excessive Use of Emergency Rooms— A large segment of the African-American population has to work during the day, and therefore they make use of the emergency rooms during the night. Furthermore, if an ill relative is left at home while others work, the emergency room becomes a doctor's office after hours! This is not an atypical example. Studies have shown that 61% of emergency room visits are unnecessary.

4. Lack of a Voice in the Decision-Making Process — This is a critical area of concern in the African-American communities relative to health care policy and delivery. This is reflected, in part, to the rapid penetration of HMOs into our communities. Their penetration, apathy, indifference, and lack of a driving force also play a role in health advocacy and are indispensable.

5. Lack of Education — This pivotal part needs immediate reconstruction from the ground up. Moreover, there must be 'preventive maintenance' on what we have and we must build upon it. Specifically, I am referring to preventive health education. Effective education programs will do much to decrease the problem areas stated above. We must get on the road to "pulling ourselves up by our boot straps," closing ranks and using what we have to our best advantage. Ultimately, our irregular edges of a fragmented health care delivery system can be transformed into an oasis of better transportation, a decrease in economic deprivity, decreased use of emergency rooms, more voice in the decision-making proves and better informed citizens, relative to preventive health education. As a result of all these changes, the entrapment of the problems should vanish.

6. Lack of Insurance— This factor strikes a mortal blow to African Americans who would seek "equal access" to health care. Quite often, being underinsured is just as devastating as being uninsured. Many health care entities and affiliates (for profit) will not cater to those who cannot pay for services. This is a fact of life! If money, -The gold standard is not there, many persons in need will suffer. Tens of millions of US Citizens, especially African Americans, are not insured. This is extricably tied to economics, e.g. employment, or the lack there of. Good jobs usually go hand in hand with good insurance coverage. There have been efforts on the national (governmental) level to broaden health care coverage, e.g. Medicare and Medicaid to pay for more services. The lack of Insurance dictates that community citizens must know where public services are available. The Health Ministry can help, tremendously, in this area.

7. Lack of Health Care Advocacy— It is generally known and accepted that politics drive this country. We must become more politically active and vigilant relative to being Advocates for Equal Access to Health Care for everyone. We do have the strength in numbers but there must be a coming together of the many community based organizations to channel the energies toward clearly defined objectives. Political advocacy can be a positive key to opening the door to equal access.

8. Lack of Self-Motivation— This part is extremely important because it invites self responsibility, lifestyle changes and behavioral modification. The questions can be pondered, e.g. what good is excellent insurance coverage if one does not avail himself/herself of the opportunity to use it. What good does it profiteth one to have the knowledge of knowing where to go for services and not having the proper motivation to seek them?

If we should begin to take charge of our own health by doing the simple things on a daily basis, e.g. walking for exercise, we could eliminate the need for expensive medical care, we must be willing to make changes in our life-styles and modify our behavior even in a radical manner, if needed. We do have a plethora of healthcare problems regarding equal access to health care, but the solution to them lies within our own communities.

The Health and Wellness Ministries in the African American church can provide the spark necessary to ignite the flame to burn the obstacles of the lack of self-motivation, unwillingness to make life-style changes and modify our behavior health wise.

The basic problem that this **Model-in-Ministry** concentrates on is twofold. They are:

1. **The lack of Preventive Health Education Awareness in the African American Church.**
2. **A need for an effective Health and Wellness Ministry in the African American Church through which the lack of Preventive Health Education Awareness can be diminished.**

We all know, explicitly, that the African American Church has been, is and always will be the bastion of hope, refuge and solace for our communities. The Black church is the stream through which things and events flow, establishing it as our cradle of information, both spiritual and otherwise. We know, further, that great things can be accomplished in and through the church!

Having said that, we now contend that the African American church is best situated to bring about the reduction of problems addressed in this book. This book's focus is to provide a reproducible Model-in-Ministry, which enables the participants to acquire basic Preventive Health Education and to increase their level of "health awareness." The fact that the focus of this book is on the African American church does not exclude linkages with other religious and ethnic institutions, e.g. health departments, etc...

This book should show overall that a Health and Wellness Ministry in the African American Church is a potentially potent vehicle for delivering Preventive Health Education awareness and helping to diminish the problems stated previously.

The existence of these problems of health crises within our communities places church pastors and church ministry workers at the forefront of the campaign to assist in their solution. Health Ministry workers, lay leaders and members are essential to the process of health care promotion.

Pastors too are unique in their position in the communities in which they serve. Their worth and prestige are legendary. I am well aware of many sick patients who call them before they call the physician. Take charge of your own health first!

It is essential that the Health and Wellness Ministry become an integral part of the overall ministries in the African American church. We conclude with the same question which we asked you to ponder initially — "Should we allow this trend of preventable diseases to continue to devastate our communities?"

This book is written to provide you — the pastors, health ministers, teachers and lay persons — with the basic knowledge to enable you to develop and initiate an effective Health and Wellness Ministry in your church.

Since health care has become one of the foundations on which we base the quality of our lives, this book should put the readers at the cutting edge of Preventive Health Care Education within the Health and Wellness Ministries in their churches.

Remember that one may be healthy (i.e.: normal blood tests, PSA., mammograms, etc.) and not be well (e.g.: physical abuse of children or parents, etc.). Health and wellness must be viewed in a holistic way — Body, Mind and Spirit — to be complete and beneficial to everyone.

Do not forget that it is cheaper to prevent disease than to cure it. Exodus 15:26 states: "If thou wilt diligently harken to the voice of the Lord, thy God, and wilt do that which is right in His sight, and will give ear to His commandments, and keep all of His statutes, I will put none of these diseases upon thee, which I have brought upon the Egyptians, for I am the Lord that healeth thee."

Please read and study this book prayerfully!

Acknowledgments

I express appreciation for their encouragement to my family: Mary, (wife); Children — Dwain (son), and (daughters) Edwina and Carla.

I wish to thank Dr. Wyatt Tee Walker, the esteemed Senior Pastor of the Canaan Baptist Church of Christ, New York City, and mentor. His wisdom, wit, humor and high intellect reign supreme.

I also thank Dr. W. Franklyn Richardson, Senior Pastor of Grace Baptist Church, Mt. Vernon, New York. He is unique in his "ready" storehouse of knowledge. I have been enriched by his in-depth understanding and insight.

My thanks to Dr. C. E. Glover, Senior Pastor, Mount Bethel Baptist Church, Fort Lauderdale, Florida, for his assistance, along with members of the congregation.

To Mrs. Sonja Fox, retired English teacher, who painstakingly and meticulously read the manuscript for this book, your contribution to this work is greatly appreciated.

A special acknowledgment and great thanks are extended to Dr. Riggins R. Earl, Jr., Ph.D., distinguished professor of Ethics and Philosophy at Interdenominational Theological Center, Atlanta, GA, for his magnificent contribution through the provocative guest introduction.

Sincere gratitude goes out to Ms. Zelma Carr who diligently served as the Mount Bethel Baptist Church's contextual representative at the oral examination for my Doctor of Ministry degree.

Letters of Acknowledgment

MEHARRY MEDICAL COLLEGE
School of Medicine
Department of Biochemistry

Edwin H. Hamilton, MD, PA
PO Box 2044
Pompano Beach, FL 33061

Dear Dr. Hamilton:
What a refreshing book!! Thank you for sharing this scholarly and compassionate work with me. I would like to purchase a copy for the libraries at Meharry Medical College and Fisk University. Students at both schools need to read this work especially if they are preparing for the health professions.
I think that my life has been enriched by knowing you and having you as a friend. You are doing so much of what I think Meharry Medical College is all about and I take great pride in telling aspiring physicians about you.
Again thank you for sharing the books. All the best to you.

Sincerely yours,
Henry A. Moses, Ph.D
1005 Dr. D.B. Todd Jr. Blvd.
Nashville, TN 37208-3599

July 25, 1999

Dr. Edwin Hamilton
2323 N.W. 19th Street
Ft. Lauderdale, FL 33311

Dear Dr. Hamilton:
Thank you for the copy of your recent publication. I am grateful for your thoughtfulness in forwarding it to me.
The book should prove valuable as a guide for congregations seeking to establish or strengthen a health and wellness ministry in as much as there is very little of such available with an African American emphasis.
You have my best wishes for a fruitful ministry.

Sincerely,
Miles J. Jones (deceased)
VIRGINIA UNION UNIVERSITY
1500 NORTH LOMBARY STREET
RICHMOND, VIRGINIA 23220

"Your original work is a great addition to the African American Church. We are praying for you my brother."

> Dr. Jeremiah Wright, Pastor
> Trinity Baptist Church of Christ
> Chicago, Illinois

The Health and Wellness Ministry in the African American Church: Preventive Health Education

By Edwin H. Hamilton, M.D., D.Min.

Unless otherwise indicated, Bible quotations are taken from the King James version of the Bible.

Guest Introduction
By
Riggins R. Earl, Jr. Ph. D.
Professor of Ethics and Theology
Interdenominational Theological Center

"When I go to church and hear people preach for hours on all kinds of subjects, especially in country districts, where the soil is fitted for growing all kinds of vegetables, all kinds of fowls, all kinds of useful shrubbery, how very much I wish the minister would take a few hours and teach the people how to fill their bodies with some of the most beautiful things with which nature has surrounded them." [1]

Washington's Perspective

Booker T. Washington uttered these words almost one hundred years ago. He spoke them to students on the campus of Tuskegee University at one of his regular Sunday evening chapel talks. Washington saw that the health condition of Black Americans, especially in the South, was in a state of national crisis. He reasoned that the Black minister ought to be more concerned about this problem. For Washington the Christian gospel spoke to the practical health needs of humanity as well as the spiritual ones. Caring for the body was necessary for the welfare of the soul and vice versa. It was for this reason that Washington assumed the task of educating the Black masses in preventive health education. He thought that Black preachers could be highly instrumental in informing the masses about the importance of good health.

Washington was impatient with Black preachers whose sermons only taught their hearers about going to heaven. He counseled that it was the job of the preacher to prepare people to live quality lives in this world. Washington lived in a day when the Black clergy suffered from a serious lack of training for leadership. He was one of the biggest constructive critics of untrained Black preachers of the twentieth century. Washington sought to help correct the problem of untrained preachers by starting an institute at Tuskegee for ministerial training. Ingeniously, Washington made practical education available to the masses. Despite his conservative politics on race, Washington's leadership contribution to the education of the Black masses must not be ignored.

Hamilton's Perspective

Dr. Hamilton's credentials in medicine and ministry are illustrative of the kind of educational progress Blacks have made in the last century. Washington could have hardly conceived of a Black preacher of his day being trained both in medicine and divinity; being a formally trained doctor of medicine and as a seminary trained doctor of ministry. Hamilton would have been a rarity. Nevertheless, Washington would have considered such professional talent invaluable to the Black community. I am confident, however, that Washington would have publically endorsed Hamilton's instructive book: **The Health and Wellness Ministry in the African American Church: Preventive Health Education.** Washington would have been attracted to the book's practical wisdom. He would have seen it as being valuable for assisting the masses of Black churches in preventive health education. Washington would resonate with Hamilton's stated purpose of the book:

This book is written to introduce and establish, throughout the African American Church, a program of Preventive Health Education through a Health and Wellness Ministry. [2]

Washington undoubtedly would have seen Hamilton's book as

being a necessary conversation piece for the Christian community. He would have seen it as being important for jump-starting a needed discussion in the Black church on the good practices of health and religion. Interestingly enough acts of good practice are the language that is used in religious circles as well as medical ones. Dr. Hamilton is both a practitioner of the science of medicine and the virtues of faith. He has struggled through the years to maintain a creative tension between reason and faith; between the discipline of the head and that of the heart. Although separated by almost a century, Washington and Hamilton seem to share common ideas about the need for exposing the Black community to preventive health education.

Readers of the book ought to know that Dr. Hamilton's passion for an informed Black community grows out of his rich experience in both medicine and the church. Hamilton wants to share with his people his medical and spiritual insights of professional practice. This is because he understands both the preacher and physician to be doing ministry. Each professional, for optimal success, must see him/herself working in partnership with God, the physician's Physician and the minister's minister, against the diseases of our bodies and souls. Daily he watches his people perish physically and spiritually for the lack of knowledge. He sees the situation of the people both with the professionally trained eyes of a medical doctor. It is no less true that Hamilton sees health challenges of people with the professionally trained vision of a Christian minister. This obviously has been one of the motivating factors behind his instructional publication. Hamilton's dual way of seeing the problem is what makes his book a trove of wisdom. It is wisdom that will assist all to a needed path of preventive health education. Hamilton wants everyone to know how to find the lifeline of opportunity for the health of our souls and bodies. He asserts in his book that Black people suffer in disproportionate numbers from preventable diseases because they too often lack knowledge. Dr Hamilton's book must be seen as carrying on the legacy of preventive health education that was formally initiated, to a large African American public, by Booker T. Washington almost a century earlier.

Booker T. Washington, because he saw the need for preventive health education, organized for his era "National Negro Health Week." He organized it under the auspices of the National Negro Business League. Washington set the date for March 21-27, 1915. Mr. Washington was very reliant upon Black church ministers as information conduits of preventive health education to this Black community. Interestingly, Washington's and Hamilton's hopes for their projects tend to resonate with each other despite the time difference that separates them as earth dwellers. Hamilton says in his book: "The writer hopes that God's people will start on their journey of diminishing the plethora of devastating diseases which plague our Black communities." Notice Hamilton's realism about the possibilities of medicine. He "hopes that God's people will start on their journey of diminishing the plethora of devastating diseases which plague our Black communities." "Diminish" is the key word here in Hamilton's description. He uses the term "diminish" rather than "destroy" intentionally. Hamilton's training in ministry and medicine would have him to know all disease will never be destroyed in the world in which we live. Less than fifty years after slavery, Booker T. Washington gives readers a dismal picture of the general health problems of Black people in the South. He admonishes his Tuskegee students at the beginning of the twentieth century:

> *"Go among the average people of our race in the South and you seldom find anybody who is well. Ask a person how he is and he will answer, 'just tolerable,' or he will tell you that he has a pain, or an ache or rheumatism-something is always wrong. Very seldom will you find anybody who can look you squarely in the face and say: 'I am well.' In nine cases out of ten, you find the body lacks the sustaining power of the good, nourishing food day by day. We have an example of this in what is called the hook-worm which we have been discussing a good deal in recent years in connection with life here in the South. The hook-worm simply means that people have not had enough to eat. Whenever you find people who have the hook-worm, they have not had enough food to eat day by day. If we could teach these people by some process how to utilize*

the food by which they are surrounded, how to utilize the plant life, how to cook their food well, how to survive well, how to make it palatable, the hook-worm would stay out of their bodies. This condition, this failure to make connection between plant life and man life not only results in ugly, weak, diseased bodies, but a weak body as you already know, means a weak mind-a mind that is not able to hold what it should hold; and a weak mind results in bad morals."

All wise leaders of the Christian faith have seen the church as the sacred house of preventive health education. Sacred knowledge about what is good for the body and the soul has been taught in the church from generation to generation. Wise leaders of the church in each generation have taught us a) what to expect from God regarding our health; b) what God expects from us regarding our health and, c) what God expects us to expect from each other regarding our health. Hamilton does not veer from that sacred wisdom's scheme of expectation. He, instead, calls upon the leaders of the church to lead us back to God's biblical norms for our good health. He wants the church to become the place where preventive health education is taught. In a word, Hamilton wants to institutionalize preventive health education in the Black church. For Hamilton the Black church is the central nervous center of the Black community.

The House of Preventive Education

This book helps us to see that the church is the house of preventive health education. Hamilton's model for ministry and wellness were crafted for use in the local church. It was one at the central nerve center of The Black community. Dr. Hamilton would readily concede that hospitals are not for preventing people from being sick. For Hamilton hospitals are for the purpose of caring for the sick. If the latter were not the case, hospitals would put themselves out of business within a short period. In comparison, the church does not exist because it can keep people from sinning. Rather, the church exists because people are sinners. The church's number one business is to teach people how they can a) prevent certain moral illnesses, and b) tell people how they can be forgiven and healed of their sin sickness. Both approaches require of us great preparation and courage. The road to communal wellness is a long rocky one. Biblically, we are taught that there are some negative things that happen to us that we, the victims, have no power to prevent. The book of Job of the New Testament is a classical attestation to that fact. For centuries the best thinkers of the church have tried to understand the intricacies of this reality. Church and science have tried to understand both the causes and consequence of diseases. The best minds of both institutions have brought their gifts to bear in their attempts at a resolution. Hamilton's book challenges church leaders to recapture the duties of teaching preventive education in the church.

Hamilton develops a model for a health and wellness ministry based upon a philosophy of disease and health derived from scriptural principles. He provides the reader with a model that he has tested in his own local membership church, the Mount Bethel Baptist Church in Ft. Lauderdale, Florida. Mount Bethel Baptist is pastored by Dr. Clarence Glover, who is a pioneering leader in his own right. Because pastor Glover is an advocate of vanguard ministries, Dr. Hamilton found the church to be an ideal ground for testing his model of wellness and ministry.

Younger pastors can benefit greatly from Hamilton's book. They might use it to pioneer for the Black church a new path for ministering to the whole person. Ministers of this persuasion will really make the Black church the house of preventive health education; the house of wholistic salvation. Good health is necessary for doing Christian ministry. Currently Black America is suffering greatly from the epidemic of AIDS. Indifference has, too often, been the church's response. Sermonic allusions to the problem is often substituted for a financed programmatic response to it. Hamilton's book provides pastors with a tested model for a programmatic development of preventive health education at the local church level. His book provides us with generic examples that pastors might use in churches of all denominations. It provides for helping pastors who are situated in both small town settings as well as large cities. Dr. Hamilton noted in the start of his book that disease has no respecter of person. It is this reality that ought to be the driving incentive for making the Black church the house of preventive health education. Imagine if we would do a better job in the Black church of harnessing our energy to minister to the health needs of each other collectively and individually? Hamilton's book provides for us a programmatic way of applying our religious beliefs about preventive health education to the lived situation. This book is for those who believe that God wants us to be healthy; that God wills the good for us. It is not for those who are trapped in their own theological arguments about what God might, or might not, want for humankind. Those of us who have problems facing the truth about our lived condition will not receive much help from this book. We must understand that God has made us responsible persons both to God's self and each other. Socially transmitted disease is an ever sobering reminder that we are so created. The church is the house that teaches corporate responsibility.

The House of Responsibility

Preventive health education ascribes to the religious belief that God made us for the world and vice versa. It is not enough to say "God made the world for us." The latter would implicate God as an overly indulging parent of God's creation. It would suggest that God has made us irresponsible. Moreover, it would say that God has spoiled us. First, let us note that God made the world for us. This is important for our understanding of having good health. The story of the book of Genesis would have us to know that God created the world before creating humanity. In that creation act, God resourced the world with those things that humanity would need for its survival. This is true even regarding medicines for our diseases. It is our disregard for acknowledging God as the resource of our existence that blinds us to this truth in most instances. Booker T. Washington was motivated by this view of God. He reminded his generation that:

"God has put into the world everything to be of value to man, to promote his happiness, to serve his purpose, and if we do not make what God has put here of the highest service to us, it will be largely our fault and the fault mainly of our failure, in most respects to take a practical, direct view of life; in a word in our failure to connect that which God has put here for our every-day life.

There is a serious gap, a serious lack, in most cases, between what God has put here and the use that we make of it, and, it seems to me that if a school of this character, or of any character has direct or practical value to the life of the people for whom it exists, one of the functions of that school should be to teach people in a direct, plain, practical manner how to take everything God has put here in this world and make it of the highest service to the people to whom that school ministers." [6]

There is always the danger of taking our religious claims from one extreme to the other. A common danger among many church people is to blame everything that happens to them on either God or the devil. Our unwillingness to take reasonable responsibility for our actions seems to be the cardinal sin of the modern world. Either we blame each other or a higher force. Christians credit the good to God; humanists generally credit the good, that they experience or accomplish, to their own ingenuity. Our failure to take responsibility for our acts too often amounts to denying the biblical truth that God made us agents of choice. That God gave us the freedom to decide is a celebrated belief among Christians. Black American Christians have a special history of struggling to exercise God's gift to them of free choice. It is what I have called in one of my own publications a body/soul dilemma. I tried to call attention to this problem in my book **Dark Symbols, Obscure Signs: God, Self, and Community in the Slave Mind**. [7] In that book, I try to show that slavery impacted Blacks' understanding of themselves anthropologically. It negatively affected the way that they thought of themselves. Slaves interpreted fragments of the Christian message that they heard from their masters to overcome a negative image of themselves as being either disembodied souls or soulless bodies.

In the last chapter of the book, I seek to show the implications of this interpretation for contemporary religious beliefs and practices. Here I make the argument that:

"Primary to the African-American theological and ethical task is the need of overcoming a gnostic view of the self that is very alive in the preaching and teaching of many black churches. I mean by a gnostic version of the self the evangelical belief that values the soul's sacredness at the expense of the body's social welfare. This view is often used as an opiate, allowing the oppressed to cope with poverty and persecution." 8

Hamilton's book ought to help Black ministers to lead Black people in partnering with God for bringing about preventive health education.

Partners in Prevention

In an informal conversation, one is subject to use the expression, "He is my partner in crime." It is a statement that usually provokes humor. The challenge in Black America is to create a church culture where we can introduce each other as partners in health prevention education. We have covenanted with God and each other for this duty. Hamilton's book provides us with the conversation themes and organizational structure for doing health prevention education in the Black church.

Preventive health education must not be only for our own congregations. Middle and upperclass Black churches must partner with churches of less economic resources for the purpose of making preventive health education accessible to the Black masses.

In the earlier years of my professional life, I had the good fortune of pastoring people who were primarily of a blue collar background. During one tenure of pastoring, I taught full-time at a major university in the area of where the church was located. It became glaringly clear for me that too many people in the church suffered from preventable and treatable health problems. These people enjoyed good worship services and the consumption of rich foods. Teaching people to change their dietary habits is not an easy task. The undeniable fact is that we are shaped by our dietary habits and vice versa. It is for this reason, perhaps, that all great religious teachers have got their followers attention by speaking to them about what they eat and drink. Understanding dietary consumption is critical to religious consciousness and vice versa. The genius of the Black Muslim leader, Elijah Mohammed, was that he helped Black people to see that they were the victim of what they ate. He convinced his followers to stop thinking like the white man by having them to stop eating the diet that slave masters forced upon their ancestors as slaves.

---

1. Booker T. Washington "A Sunday Evening Talk [Tuskegee, Ala.] March 27, 1910" in The Booker T. Washington Papers volume 10: 1909-11. Louis R. Harlan and Raymond W. Smock, Editors (Urbana: University of Illinois Press 1981), p. 301.

2. Edwin Harvey Hamilton The Health and Wellness Ministry in the African American Church: Preventive Health Education (Winter Park, Florida: Four-G Publishers, Inc. 1999), preface iv.

3. Washington, Op. Cite. volume 13, p. 218.

4. Ibid.

5. Washington, Op. Cite. volume 10, p. 10-11.

6. Washington, Op. Cite., p. 298-99

7. Dark symbols, Obscure Signs: God, Self, and Community in the Slave Mind (Maryknoll, New York: Orbis 1993)

8. Riggins R. Earl, Jr., Dark Symbols, Obscure Signs: God, Self, and Community in the Slave Mind (Maryknoll, New York: Orbis Books 1995), p. 161.

Chapter One

THE THEORETICAL FOUNDATION FOR THE HEALTH AND WELLNESS MINISTRY

To be thorough in regards to the problems and to understand their theoretical foundations, it is imperative that we are comprehensive in their examination. This is done to facilitate their resolution. This author, therefore, examines the problems from the several perspectives, namely: Theological-Biblical, Historical, Sociological, Traditional, Economical, Educational and Practical.

The problem re-stated is: 1) there is a lack of Preventive Health Education in the African American Church; 2) there is a critical need for an effective Health and Wellness Ministry in the African American Church through which the overall health of its members and their families can be improved.

THE THEOLOGICAL-BIBLICAL PERSPECTIVE

From this perspective, it can be stated that God, our Father: the Creator and Redeemer of humankind has given us innumerable opportunities for redemption. This has been occurring since the fall of Adam and Eve in the Garden of Eden (Genesis 3). Because of pride and rebellion, they sinned and disobeyed the word of God.

Their preventive health education instructions were as follows:

> *"But of the fruit of the tree, which is in the midst of the Garden, God hath said, ye shall not eat of it, lest ye die."*
> **Genesis 2:17 KJV**

Humankind has been sinning, missing the mark and violating God's commands, since the fall in the garden. This refers to His commands in general and to those pertaining to our bodies, specifically **("the fruit of a tree yielding seed; to you it shall be for food." Genesis. 1:29 KJV)**

> *"The fruit of the tree...ye shall not eat of it...lest ye die"*
> Genesis 2:17 KJV

Despite this, through His redemptive goodwill, God has allowed us to survive despite our iniquities.

The Dietary Laws of Deuteronomy 14:4 - 9 and 20 KJV admonished us as to what we should eat.

> Verse 4: *"These are the beasts which ye shall eat: the ox, the sheep and the goat."*

> Verse 7: *"Nevertheless these ye shall not eat of them that chew the cud."*

> Verse 8: *"And the swine ..."*

These foods (swine - pig/hog) when eaten, contribute to our unhealthy states, e.g. hypercholesterolemia (increased levels of blood cholesterol-fat). We are forbidden to eat foods that contribute to the destruction of our bodies.

> Verse 9: *"These shall ye eat of all that are in the waters: all that have fins and scales shall ye eat."*

It is an established medical fact that fish with scales and fins are nutritious and wholesome.

> Verse 20: *"But of all clean fowls ye may eat."* Chicken and turkey are healthy and should be eaten, **without the skin.**

It is understood that even though the Dietary Laws were written in the Old Testament, Deuteronomy, chapter 14:3-26, the instructions should be followed by all to this day. This is in our best interests medically and healthwise.

Paul writes in Romans, 14:1-12 regarding the Christian and debatable things in reference to the principle of individual responsibility. This helps one to avert the absolute sense of legalization implied in Deuteronomy chapter 14:3-23.

> Paul gives further amplification in Romans 14:2-3.
> *"For one believeth that he may eat all things; another, who is weak, eateth herbs."*
>
> *"Let not him that eateth despise him that eateth not; and let not him who eateth not judge him that eateth; for God hath received him."*

The question is, can one eat those harmful foods written about in Deuteronomy 14? The ready answer is a resounding yes! On the other hand, we should not eat them because they are harmful (unhealthy) to our bodies (e.g. swine should not be eaten).

> *"Do not destroy the work of God for the sake of food. All things indeed are pure, but it is evil for the man/woman who eats with offense."* Romans 14:20

Despite the above, humankind eats those foods which are deleterious to their bodies and health. Hence, **Preventive Health Education** needs more emphasis in the African American Church.

There is a glimpse of a Biblical foundation for the establishment of a Health and Wellness Ministry. In Genesis 43:16 and following KJV, Joseph was found entertaining his eleven brothers.

More specifically, Verses 27 and 28 give us more in-depth illumination into that ministry. This gives us a glimpse of a Health and Wellness Ministry.

> Verse 27: *"And he asked them of their **welfare** and said, Is your father well, the old man of whom ye spoke? Is he yet alive?"*

Here Joseph asked his brothers of their **welfare**. He also asked, *"Is your father well?"*
Verse 28: And they answered, *"Thy servant our father is in **good health**, he is yet alive." And they bowed down their heads and made obeisance. Here they answered saying, "Thy servant our father is in **good health**."*

Very early in Genesis, health and welfare were of concern to Joseph. It is to be noted that the Hebrew word shalom means "wholeness" as well as "peace." In him we glimpse a minister of Health and Wellness. To further illustrate and make clear the meaning of a minister of Health and Wellness (Health Ministry) let us look at the raising of the Shunamite woman's son from the dead by Elisha. This was the initial case of CPR (Cardiopulmonary Resuscitation) recorded in Holy Writ.

> *"And he went up and lay upon the child, and put his **mouth upon his mouth**, and his eyes upon his eyes and his hands upon his hands; and he stretched himself upon the child; and the flesh of the child became warm."*
> 2 Kings 4:34, KJV
> 19
> *"Then he returned and walked in the house to and fro, and went up and stretched himself upon him; and the child sneezed seven times, and the child opened his eyes."*
> 2 Kings 4:35 KJV

This Biblical account of CPR was simple, direct, efficient and powerful. Though Elisha physically revived the child, there wasn't any doubt that Divine intervention was there because all healing is of God. This record gave us another glimpse of a Minister of Health and Wellness (Health Ministry).

The aforementioned incidents assist in explaining the early development of a Health Ministry.

God as the Creator and Redeemer of humankind, in His infinite wisdom and omniscience, sent His son Jesus Christ to us. He was sent as the quintessential Health Minister with an incomparable Health Ministry.

> Jesus declared in Luke 4:18 KJV: *"The spirit of the Lord is upon me, because he hath anointed me to preach the **gospel to the poor**, he hath sent me to heal the brokenhearted to preach deliverance to the captives and recovering of sight to the blind, to set at liberty them that are bruised."*

Jesus was constantly in the company of the poor-"the least of these"-who were disadvantaged, hopeless and hapless.

He made it clear that the Spirit of the Lord was upon him, and that he was anointed to preach the good news to the poor. These included large segments of African Americans. These are they who comprise the writer's medical practice and context today. Their stations in life range from the poverty line and below. The poor in poverty tend to breed envy and hatred leading to crime and brokenheartedness. Moreover there was recovery of sight to the blind-the physical (by Jesus).

The message of Luke 4:18 KJV is directed to the people of God and His Church. Implicit in Jesus' ministry there is health and wellness, e.g. the healing of the brokenhearted and recovering the sight of the blind.

The Health and Wellness Ministry should be a stimulus for the setting free of individuals from the slavery of ignorance and those harmful activities that make for bad health. As we do the work of the ministry we are actually bearing each other's burdens (Galatians 6:2 KJV).

Through Jesus Christ, churches are empowered to carry on effective Health and Wellness Ministries. The central basis for the essence of this Health and Wellness Ministry is found in a key question asked by Saint Paul in 1 Corinthians, 6:19 KJV:

"What? Know ye not that your body is the temple of the Holy Spirit who is in you, whom ye have of God, and ye are not your own.?"

This scripture is truly applicable to us and to the understanding of our bodies relative to the Health Ministry.

> *"There is a dignity and service of the body. Some consideration may commend the sanctification of the flesh to God. The natural care of our bodies should be evident. The idea of the temple implies the presence of God. Therefore, if the body be the temple of the Holy Spirit it should follow that He is actually there. It should be understood that the utilization of our bodies to God is because He assumes such is the case. This is rather than us rendering to Him the body's use out of courtesy. Our bodies should be watched jealously. The body is His because we were bought with a price. Respect for the body, because it is the temple of the Holy Spirit, should teach us how to dress and how we view our bodily appearance. For example, we may follow the drunkard who would abuse his/her natural health by sin with the resultant bodily neglect. But once his/her heart has been changed by God, a noticeable difference is evident. His/her place is then taken among humankind. We need to be cognizant of all our habits with the ultimate end that our bodies be in the best shape to do the will of God."*

1. Joseph S. Excell, The Biblical Illustrator, I Corinthians, Chapter VI (Grand Rapids, Michigan, Baker Book House 1964) 427.

It follows that this is the highest objective of health. We know that Christ is manifested in a body, furthermore, much of His teaching was about the body and many of His miracles were performed primarily on the body. This further makes clear the healing ministry of Jesus Christ. We know that the **body**, the **mind and the spirit** have a close connection.

The state of one can affect the condition of the other and the body does coincide with humankind's inner life. If we would recognize that the person is **"a temple"** then our dealings with our brothers and sisters should take on new meaning. This would be true despite how educated, illiterate, wicked, poor or rich one may be. Surely none of us would knowingly desecrate the **"temple of the Holy Spirit"**-our bodies. The question can legitimately be asked, What right has any man or any women to deface the temple of the Holy Spirit? (Our bodies are so wonderful that God names His own attributes after parts of them. His omniscience-it is God's eye. His omnipresence-it is God's ear. His omnipotence-it is God's arm.)

In summary, the sanctity of the body is to be respected because it is God's temple.

First Corinthians 6:19 KJV and its implications were used for the teaching and doing the ministry based on the premise that "the body is the temple of the Holy Spirit." We were bought with a price and we are not our own. We belong to God. This verse of scripture helps to undergird what the theological focus of the ministry is all about. Christians should be taught the true significance theologically of 1 Corinthians 6:19 KJV relative to their bodies being **the temple of the Holy Spirit**. When this is done in association with health issues (diseases, etcetera) we should be empowered to do more to keep our bodies-the temple of the Holy Spirit-healthy.

"Now unto Him that is able to keep you from falling..."
Jude 24 KJV

Having stated the above, this writer sincerely believes that God would have His Health Ministry guided by the fore stated scriptures.

THE HEALTH ACADEMY: ITS NEED, PURPOSE AND COMPOSITION

THE NEED - There is a dire need for children, in their formative years, to know the general nature of preventative health measures and the things that could be done to prevent many diseases.

THE PURPOSE - The purpose of the Health Academy is to fulfill the need by teaching children the vital importance of maintaining healthy bodies. This includes proper exercise, dieting and not smoking. They should be taught the importance of ecology and our environment, e.g. clean air and water, among others.

THE COMPOSITION - The Health Academy is composed of young children from the ages five years through high school. Members of that Academy are called "Health Disciples."
A new and innovative component called the Health Academy is hereby instituted. It had not been done before according to the literature. They are taught the importance of health and healthy lifestyles.

THE GOAL - The goal of the Health Academy is to actively raise their level of **Preventive Health Education** to an unprecedented high level.

The Christian Lecture Series is undergirded by:
"Study to show thyself approved unto God a workman that needeth not to be ashamed rightly dividing the word of truth."
2 Timothy 2:15 KJV

The Holistic component of **The Christian Lecture Series** is composed of the **Body, Mind and Spirit**. Scriptures which undergird it are:

THE BODY - *"I beseech you therefore, brethren by the mercies of God, that you present your bodies a living sacrifice, holy, acceptable unto God, which is your reasonable service."*

Romans 12:1 KJV

THE MIND - *"For God hath not given us the spirit of fear, but of power, and of love, and of a sound mind."* 2 Timothy 1:9 KJV

THE SPIRIT - *"But ye are not in the flesh but in the Spirit, if so be that the Spirit of God dwell in you. Now if any man/woman have not the Spirit of Christ he/she is none of His."* Romans 8:9 KJV

The above was demonstrated by noted psychiatrist Freda Lewis Hall, M.D. She spoke on "Depression in the African American Community" on Health Sunday October 20, 1997 after the Annual Health Fair. The lecture was held at Mount Bethel Baptist Church in Fort Lauderdale, Florida.

THE HISTORICAL PERSPECTIVE

The Black Church was known to have placed very little emphasis on health promotion, especially Preventive Health Education. To the writer's best recollection, the closest thing to a Health Ministry has been the Nurses Guild. It was composed of women who were not necessarily nurses at all. They were there, during Church services, to help. They were those who expressed a desire to serve, whether they had training as Registered Nurses, Licensed Practical Nurses or someone who just made beds in a hospital or nursing home. "The desire to be" and to help those in need were more important than training. The women were always beautifully attired in white nurses uniforms. They were always under the direct control of the pastor. They were there during church services to help those who shouted, primarily. Their paraphernalia were composed of two things: one physical-"a Church hand fan"-and two, a bottle of smelling salts (an aromatic preparation used as a stimulant and restorative to relieve faintness).

The nurses would be stationed strategically around church pews, poised for action. At the height of the preacher's sermon, when emotions and the spiritual crescendo reached their zenith, they would immediately proceed to function. "Shouting" (uncontrolled body movement associated with varying sounds of different decibels) usually provoked the response of the nurses. A minor shout or the possibility of a major one would bring the church hand fans into play. The nurses would immediately "fan" the person to allay the full blown shout. They usually knew the members, of the congregation who were more prone to shout. This knowledge brought the proper piece of equipment to the scene.

No doubt when there was a full-blown "shout" all paraphernalia were utilized, e.g. the fan (used vigorously) and the smelling salts, to ward off the total collapse of the member. In those cases, two to four nurses participated. Members of the usher board usually helped out. This writer never saw any blood pressure checks, etcetera being done during those days. There was no community health outreach.

The foregoing description is the extent of the traditional Nurses Guild in the African American Church, to the writer's best recollection. Community Health Outreach was foreign to their mission. They were, in essence, similar to Phoebe, servant (deaconess) of the Church (Romans 16:1 KJV). She was a helper of many. They- Nurses Guilds-did play a key role with their participation in services. Theirs was the first line of care.

THE SOCIOLOGICAL PERSPECTIVE

Sociologically speaking, it is believed that the problem of the lack of preventive health care is impacted by human society. This holds true, especially for African Americans. Their needs are felt to be minimal or nonexistent in relation to other ethic groups. Regarding health care and disease prevention, we are not afforded the basic accessible health care, though health care facilities abound in our society. An effective vehicle to assist in alleviating the problem is the Health and Wellness Ministry in the African American Church. African Americans-"the least of these"-were victimized by the vicious perpetuation of a biased system of health care. All elements available to us are needed to address the problem set forth in this book. This writer concludes that the proper utilization of our Health Ministries helps to diminish an ongoing problem though Preventive Health Education.

THE TRADITIONAL PERSPECTIVE

Much of what happened to us relative to the Health Ministry was handed down. We became victims of cyclical behavior in regards to what happened to us in our church ministries. Since we were not taught anything about Preventive Health Education and a Health Ministry, there had not been any appreciable change in us. This author knows that the emphasis has to be changed in order to help diminish the problem.

THE ECONOMICAL PERSPECTIVE

African Americans have less money to spend. Their per capita income is lower than other ethnic groups in America. Medical insurance coverage is difficult, if not impossible, to obtain. They have to work during the day and use the hospital emergency rooms for doctors' offices at night. In many instances it has been difficult for us to pay for the bare necessities of life. Further, our reliance on public transportation added to the problem. Yet, Preventive Health Education does not pose a tremendously burdensome problem relative to capital outlay. The Health Ministry can help to diminish the lack of Preventive Health Education through a Health and Wellness Ministry. And, for the most part, this can be done without a financial donation of any kind. The willingness to serve and contribute are major factors in that Ministry.

THE EDUCATIONAL PERSPECTIVE

In general, we African Americans are less informed relative to our health needs than other ethnic groups. What is available to them has been practically nonexistent for us. It is well known that having knowledge was one thing but being motivated to use that knowledge is quite different. Emphasis must be placed on one's responsibility for his/her own health. The importance of taking charge of one's health is also stressed. In summary, the scriptures describe for us how God is cognizant of Preventive Health Education. He told humankind (Adam and Eve) not to eat of the fruit in the midst of the garden (Genesis 3:3 KJV). This was his verbal order (prescription). There are certain foods which are not good for us. Dietary laws relative to what we should eat are as true today as they were in the Old Testament. For example, we were told not to eat swine (Deuteronomy 14 KJV).

Additionally, glimpses of the Health Ministry were demonstrated in the persons of Joseph (Genesis 43:27 & 28 KJV) and Elisha (2 Kings 4:34 & 35 KJV).

Since the body is viewed as the temple of the Holy Spirit, it goes without saying that we are to treat it with care. It is not to be desecrated. We were entrusted to care for our bodies. God, our Creator and Redeemer of humankind, in His infinite wisdom and omniscience, sent His son Jesus Christ to us as the example of a Health Minister (Luke 4:18 KJV). We, the people of God-The Church-are charged with the responsibility of continuing the work set forth by Jesus Christ (Luke 4:18 KJV) in our Health and Wellness Ministry (e.g. Preventive Health Education).

THE PRACTICAL PERSPECTIVE

The perspectives stated above are important in explaining the theoretical foundation but the practical one is most important. This is true because the ministry model must be duplicated and utilized in the "real world." What has been said was of practical value, e.g. the Bible's teachings on Preventive Health Education and Dietary Laws. These teachings are as true today as they were when first stated in the Bible. The problem, as previously identified, should be resolved by the design and implementation of the three part Health and Wellness Ministry Model. The expected result is an increase in Preventive Health Education Awareness.

The Health and Wellness Ministry
in the African American Church
Preventive Health Education

Health Academy Suggested Youth Questionnaire

(Pre-test and Post-test)

1. What is Health? _____
_____
_____
_____

2. What is the Health Academy? _____
_____
_____
_____

3. What is a Health Disciple? _____
_____
_____
_____

4. What are the dangers of smoking cigarettes? _____
_____
_____
_____

The Health and Wellness Ministry in the African American Church

5. What is the importance of regular exercise? Do you exercise regularly? _____
_____
_____
_____

6. What is the value of a healthy diet?_____
_____
_____
_____

7. Why is it important to read the labels on the foods in the store?
_____
_____
_____

8. What is Ecology?_____
_____
_____
_____

9. What are the dangers of drinking alcohol and what are the dangers of using drugs? _____
_____
_____
_____

10. What is the Bible saying about your body and the Holy Spirit?
_____
_____
_____

The Health and Wellness Ministry in the African American Church Preventive Health Education

Health Academy
Answers to Questionnaire

1. Health is freedom from disease, pain and defect. _____
   _____
   _____

2. The Health Academy is a group of children, five years of age through high school. _____
   _____
   _____

3. The Health Disciples are members of the Health Academy. They are learners of healthy living _____
   _____
   _____

4. The dangers of smoking are lung cancer and lung diseases.
   _____
   _____

5. Regular exercise helps to keep your bodies strong, healthy and prevents some diseases. _____
   _____
   _____

6. A healthy diet supplies your bodies with the necessary protein, carbohydrates, and fats. Vitamins are also important. _____
   _____
   _____

7. Labels tell us what is in food we eat. We will know those foods that should not be eaten. _____
_____
_____

8. Ecology is the study of the human being and the environment.
_____
_____

9. Drinking alcohol leads to liver disease and the use of drugs blocks our minds and keeps us from being normal. _____
_____
_____

10. "Know ye not that your body is the temple of the Holy Spirit.? I Corinthians 6:19 _____
_____
_____.

The Health and Wellness Ministry in the African American Church Preventive Health Education
Adult Questionnaire
(Pre-test and Post-test)

1. Do you believe at this time that Preventive Health Education is essential to you as a Christian? (Check only one) ❏ YES ❏ NO

2. Do you know what the Bible is saying specifically about your body and the Holy Spirit? (Check only one) ❏ YES ❏ NO

If known, please give the scriptural reference(s). _____
_____
_____
_____

3. Is there a need for you to become more health conscious, more self-responsible, change your lifestyle and help you take charge of your health? (Check only one) ❏ YES ❏ NO

4. Do you know of any scripture(s) or Biblical references related to the Health and Wellness Ministry?
(Check only one) ❏ YES ❏ NO
If known, please give the scriptural reference(s) _____
_____
_____
_____

5. Do you believe that there is a need for the Faith Community (churches) to form linkages with local Health Departments? (Check only one) ❏ YES ❏ NO

6. Is there a need for our youth to be taught the Biblical importance of Preventive Health Education principles and advantages of healthy lifestyles? (Check only one) ❏ YES ❏ NO

7. Do you know that African American men have the world's highest incidence of Prostate Cancer and mortality (death rate)-it kills more Black men than other male population? (Check only one) ❏ YES ❏ NO

8. Are you aware of any screening tests for Prostate Cancer? (Check only one) ❏ YES ❏ NO

9. Do you see a Community Health Fair as being a positive part of the Health and Wellness Ministry in Community Health Outreach? (Check only one) ❏ YES ❏ NO

10. What is your present view of the place of the Health and Wellness Ministry in the Church? (Check only one)
❏ HAVE NO OPINION
❏ IT SHOULD NOT EXIST
❏ IT IS ESSENTIAL TO MY LIFE AS A CHRISTIAN
❏ I COULD DO WELL WITHOUT IT

Chapter Two

Methodology
Model-In-Ministry Design

This is a simple, three component, **Model-in-Ministry** which is easily remembered, duplicated and implemented in Any Church, Any Community, USA.

In summary, the objectives are to 1.) effectively increase Preventive Health Education, 2.) establish a Health and Wellness Ministry Model, and 3.) teach some Biblical principles to our youth in the Health Academy. In addition, the Community Health Outreach which is exemplified by the Community Health Fair.

The basic problem addressed by this model has been clearly delineated previously. The problem had its genesis in the author's observations in religious circles (churches, etcetera) and his extensive medical practice in the African American community for more than three decades. His experience with multiple devastating diseases, many of which could be averted by effective Preventive Health Education, anchored this author's mind-set.

This **Model-In-Ministry** is designed with three major components. They are:
1. **THE MINISTER OF HEALTH AND WELLNESS**
2. **PREVENTIVE HEALTH EDUCATION AND**
3. **COMMUNITY HEALTH OUTREACH**

The structure, as stated, helps to facilitate one's overall understanding of the ministry, the result of which makes for better memory retention. The three major components are interrelated.

The Minister of Health and Wellness in this model is a physician (M.D.). That does not preclude one of several other medical persons or laity from holding the position.

Preventive Health Education is the content of the teaching sessions of the ministry on a periodic basis.

Community Health Outreach is that which extends into the overall community outside of the local church congregation. The prime example of this is the Annual Community Health Fair. The collaboration of several churches (interfaith linkages) and the local Health Department increases its impact and success.

It is to be understood clearly that the Annual Community Health Fair is not to preclude churches from having their own Mini Health Fairs.

The Church Pastor is an ex officio member of the Health Ministry.

The Health Academy with its Health Disciples consists of children aged five years through high school.

A pre-test (Questionnaire) is administered before the sessions are taught. The same test is given after the sessions have been taught in order to assess the effectiveness, relative to the increase of Preventive Health Education through the Health and Wellness Ministry. An interactive question and answer period is allowed after each session.

The children, aged 5 years through high school, are taught in the Health Academy. The participants are called Health Disciples. Three one hour sessions are held. Pre-test and post-test questionnaires are administered. All relevant subject matter is covered. Interactive post session question and answer periods are conducted.

The Health and Wellness Ministry in the African American Church Preventive Health Education

Organizational Flow Chart
(The Basic Health and Wellness Ministry Structure)

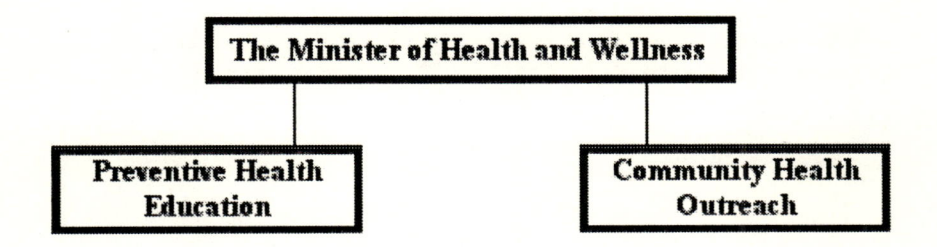

```
         The Minister of Health and Wellness
          |                              |
   Preventive Health             Community Health
      Education                      Outreach
```

DETAILED ORGANIZATIONAL DESIGN FOR A BASIC HEALTH AND WELLNESS MINISTRY

THE MINISTER OF HEALTH AND WELLNESS
(Medical Director)
Administrative & Teaching
Corps of Volunteers
Laity Training
Church Pastor - Ex Officio Member

PREVENTIVE HEALTH EDUCATION

Exercise
Diet Control
Periodic Health Screenings
Holistic: Body-Mind-Spirit
Health Academy—
Health Disciples (Youth)

COMMUNITY HEALTH OUTREACH

Annual Community Health Fair
Linkages to Local Health Dept.
Christian Health Lecture Series
Holistic: Body-Mind-Spirit
Periodic Health Screenings

Chapter Three

Planning the Health and Wellness Ministry

This present day structure of the Health Ministry (now called the Health and Wellness Ministry) is broader in scope and more inclusive in its programs and outreach. This has evolved primarily from the diversity and needs of the congregation and society. Initially, the ministry was called the Health and Welfare Ministry. Today it is called the Health and Wellness Ministry. The word "welfare" was dropped because of its negative connotations in some circles. The "wellness" was added because it provokes a more positive attitude and mind-set relative to being healthy.

From a Biblical standpoint, in Genesis 43:27 and 28, Joseph is found asking about his brother's welfare, (verse 27) and their response to health (verse 28).

> Verse 27-"And he asked them of their welfare, and said, Is your father well, the old man of whom he spoke? Is he yet alive?"
>
> Verse 28-"And they answered, Thy servant our father, is in good health, he is yet alive. And they bowed down their heads, and made obeisance."

It is God's plan that the welfare and health of all His saints are predominantly part of His ministry in regards to the church's mission in the world. One can readily see that the mention of Health and Wellness goes back to our Old Testament days. Specifically, Joseph asked of his brother's welfare in Genesis 43:27 and their response to health in verse 28.

There is also some theological foundation for the ministry in the New Testament. In First Corinthians Chapter 6, verse 19, we find Paul asking a question: *"What? Know ye not that your body is the temple of the Holy Spirit who is in you, whom ye have of God and ye are not on your own?"*

The sanctity of the body is emphasized and it is God's temple. Jesus, Himself, healed many of diverse diseases.

This ministry has been viewed as an isolated entity, in some instances, rather than as an important part of the total ministries in the Church. An isolated ministry in the Church is very ineffective and serves no total useful purpose in furthering God's program on earth. By this, the author means in a theological sense regarding the mission of the Church in the world.

The Health and Wellness Ministry, as it is structured at Mount Bethel Church, is new, innovative, and very different from the traditional Nurses Guild as has been stated previously. There is interest generated in the local congregation.

The ministry is primarily one of servanthood-giving of one's self as a Christian to expand the Kingdom of God through service to mankind.

> *"Give, and it shall be given unto you, good measure, pressed down and shaken together, and running over, shall men give unto your bosom. For with the same measure it shall be measured to you again."*
> St. Luke 6:38 KJV

The above scripture aptly explains and helps to set the tone of the Health and Wellness Ministry. The total health and wellness of the human being (both physical and spiritual) is what we are primarily concerned with in this ministry.

Jesus sets the tone for this ministry. In St. Luke 4:18, Jesus declared that:

> *"The Spirit of the Lord is upon me, because He hath anointed me to preach the gospel to the poor; He hath sent me to heal the brokenhearted, to preach deliverance to the captives, and recovering of sight to the blind, to set at liberty them that are bruised."*

The body (physical), mind (mental) and spirit and encompassed in the above scripture.

For one to grasp the significance of the human body, theologically, we must go again to the Holy Bible.

> *"What? Know ye not that your body is the temple of the Holy Spirit who is in you, whom ye have of God, and ye are not your own?"*
> 1 Corinthians 6:19

The sanctity of the human body is to be respected because it is God's temple. We are not our own. This verse of scripture undergirds what the theological focus of the ministry is all about. Christians should be taught the true significance theologically of 1 Corinthians 6:19 relative to their bodies being the temple of the Holy Spirit. When this is done in association with health issues (diseases, etcetera), we should be able to do more to keep our bodies, "God's Temple," healthy.

The Minister of Health and Wellness

The Minister of Health and Wellness may be male or female. This person may be professional, paraprofessional or laity. He or she may be a Physician (M.D.), Osteopathic Physician (D.O.), Dentist, Registered Nurse, Licensed Practical Nurse, Medical Technician, or a person from the general laity.

The Minister of Health must be dedicated and committed to the

Ministry, wholeheartedly. He or she is extremely critical to the effectiveness of the ministry.

The eventual selection of this person rests with the Pastor.

To further elucidate and illustrate the meaning of a Minister of Health, let us look at Elisha's raising of the Shunamites woman's son from the dead. This was the initial case of CPR (cardiopulmonary resuscitation) recorded in the Bible.

> *"And he went up and lay upon the child, and put his mouth upon his mouth, and his eyes upon his eyes and his hands upon his hand; and the flesh of the child became warm."*
> II Kings 4:35

> *"Then he returned, and walked in the house to and fro, and went up and stretched himself upon him: and the child sneezed seven times, and the child opened his eyes."*
> II Kings 4:35

The Biblical account of CPR was simple, direct, efficient and powerful.

The Corps of Volunteers

This group is comprised of males and females, children and adults. They come from the congregation in general and everyone is welcome. Persons do not have to be medically or paramedically trained. This is true because a very diversified and multi-talented group is needed.

The Laity Training

The goal here is the training of laity who train others. This training is done by facilitating the ready dissemination of information which helps to ensure a replicable model of ministry. Trainers and trainees are children and adults.

The holistic approach is fully utilized and is of primary importance. It is of significance, especially relative to Preventive Health Education in this ministry.

The total concept of God's temple (your body) is critical to your understanding of this component of the ministry.

You may meditate again on the core of the scripture for this ministry:

> *"What? Know ye not that your body is the temple of the Holy Spirit who is in you, whom ye have of God, and ye are not your own?"*
> 1 Corinthians 6:19

Remember that the body as we think of it, is more than two hundred and six bones, sixty trillion cells, muscles, nerves, skin, and chemicals-water, salt, etcetera. In addition to these components, the body has a mind and a spirit; therefore, one must view it holistically. This means that the holistic concept is the Body, Mind and Spirit. For example, the mental illness depression typifies the holistic viewpoint relative to diseases.

Depression is rampant in the African American community and must be treated as a disease, the same as hypertension (high blood pressure) and diabetes (sugar) rather than in an isolated or disjointed fashion because its true value will be missed. Look upon the body as a whole, with many parts.

Scriptural Meditations for the Holistic Components The Body-

> *"I beseech you therefore, brethren, by the mercies of God, that you present your bodies a living sacrifice, holy, acceptable unto God, which is your reasonable service."*
> Romans 12:1 KJV

We must be ready to present our bodies-"God's Temples"-to

God in a Holy fashion which is our minimum duty. We should not desecrate God's Temple with ungodly treatments, e.g. eating unhealthy foods or not exercising regularly.

The Mind-

"For God hath not given us the spirit of fear but of power, and of love, and of a sound mind."
2 Timothy 1:7 KJV

The above was demonstrated by noted psychiatrist, Freda Lewis Hall, M.D.. She spoke on Depression in the African American Community.

The Spirit-

"But ye are not in the flesh but in the spirit, if so be that the Spirit of God dwell in you. Now if any man/woman have not the Spirit of Christ, he/she is none of His."
Romans 8:9 KJV

This affords us the tranquility that we need to keep our bodies "temples of the Holy Spirit" functioning daily together with the "Spirit of God."

THE HEALTH ACADEMY - HEALTH DISCIPLES (YOUTH)

The concept of the Health Academy is innovative and its worth and implications are extremely important for our optimum Health and Wellness: Preventive Health Education now and in the future.

THE NEED

There is an urgently dire need for children in their formative years to know the general nature of **Preventive Health Education** concepts and the things that should be done to prevent many diseases. Inherent in this is also the need to maintain healthy bodies. It is also clear the early Preventive Health Education and promotion help to decrease chronic debilitating diseases in later years.

THE PURPOSE

The purpose of the Health Academy is to fulfill the need as stated previously by teaching children the vital importance of maintaining healthy bodies. The teaching includes the value of proper exercising, dieting, and the dangers of smoking.

They are taught the important parts about ecology (the branch of biology that deals with the relations between living organisms and their environment) e.g. clean air and water.

The goal is to raise their conscious level of **Preventive Health Education Awareness** to unprecedented heights.

THE COMPOSITION

The Health Academy should be composed of children from the ages of five years through high school. Members of this academy are called "Health Disciples." You may develop your own guidelines regarding the age limits. What the author has given is only a guide.

THE IMPLEMENTATION

Through the active participation of the Health Disciples, there are structured teaching sessions on pertinent themes as follows: exercise, healthy diet, dangers of smoking, dangers of unhealthy lifestyles, and the subject of ecology, to include education about the environment.

Examples of a ten-question pre-test (before teaching) and a post-test (after teaching) that should be given to the disciples in the Health Academy, along with answers, are found at the end of chapter one.

This is an extremely exciting program with potential to help diminish the continuing ever-increasing spiral of devastating diseases and environmentally harmful conditions in the African American community.

Biblical Undergirdings

The Biblical undergirdings for the significant relevance of the Health Academy Disciples are:

Scriptural Meditations for the Health Academy Health Disciples

General theme (Core Scripture)

"Train up a child in the way he/she should go and when he/she is old, he/she will not depart from it." Proverbs 22:6 KJV

"And ye, fathers provoke not your children unto wrath, but bring them up in the nurture and admonition of the Lord." Ephesians 6:4 KJV

"For children are a heritage from the Lord." Psalms 127:3 KJV

Just as early detection is key to adequate treatment of diseases, our children must be trained-healthwise-in the way they should go and when they are older, they will not depart from it. Our true future lies here if we are ever to make significant strides toward better health in our communities.

Valuable Scriptures for Sessions on Sex Education

"But for fornication, and all uncleanness, or covetousness, let it not be once named among you as becometh saints."
Ephesians 5:3 KJV

"For we know that no fornicator or unclean person nor covetous man/woman (who is an idolater) hath any inheritance in the kingdom of Christ and of God."
Ephesians 5:5 KJV

It is a fact of life that our young children get involved with peers and become victims to the dangers of teenage pregnancy and its harmful consequences. The Church, through the Health Academy and Health Disciples, undergirded by God's Holy Word, can do much to stop this unfortunate plague in our communities. Professional help (inside and/or outside) can be solicited and utilized in the most important aspect of the ministry. We must act!

Valuable Scriptures for Sessions on Conduct

"Neither filthiness foolish talking, nor jesting, which are not convenient (fitting), but, rather, giving of thanks."
Ephesians 5:4 KJV

This is needed for the Holistic Component (approach)-Body - Mind - Spirit.

The children's minds must be elevated above common expression which tends to be ungodly. It is to be understood that our salvation healthwise lies within our present community resources.

EXERCISE

The first segment of Preventive Health Education is Exercise. It has been shown, for example, that exercise, control of one's blood pressure and not eating fat can do much to decrease the incidence of heart disease. The exercise will have to be tailored to the individuals needs, e.g. : + age, aerobics, line dancing. Before one embarks on a program of exercise, he/she should be examined by a physician, especially if he/she is a senior citizen. Exercise, to be effective, must be done on a consistent basis. This true whether the work-out is walking, jogging or running, etcetera.

Jazzercize or aerobics is one activity to incorporate into the ministry's exercise program. Survey the congregation for member(s) who may have expertise in this area.

Exercise will help to give you a sense of well-being

Points to remember about exercise:
1. The purpose of exercise is to strengthen the body and prevent its undue deterioration.

2. Proper exercise goes hand in hand with proper diet.

3. The "right frame of mind" is critical for success when exercising.

4. The exercise must be tailored to the individual's needs.

5. Consider medical conditions before exercising.

6. Consult your physician for a physical examination before exercising, especially senior-citizens.

7. Exercise regularly, e.g. three times a week etcetera. Remember that consistency in short periods of exercise is more beneficial than infrequent longer periods of time.

Note: The Minister of Health and Wellness should have a person qualified to come and give specific instructions regarding exercise.

Scriptural Meditations for Exercise

> *"Lord, my heart is not haughty, nor mine eyes lofty; Neither do I exercise myself in great matters, or in things too high for me."*
> Psalms 131:1 KJV

> *"I exercise myself to have always a conscience void of offense toward God and toward men."*
> The Acts 24:16 KJV

> *"Exercise thyself rather unto godliness."*
> I Timothy 4:7 KJV

> *"But strong meat (solid food) belongeth to them that are of full age, even those who by reason of use have their senses exercised to discern both good and evil."*
> Hebrews 5:14 KJV

> *"Seest thou how faith wrought upon with his works, and by works was faith made perfect."*
> James 2:22 KJV

Diet Control

Good diet control stands at the forefront of Preventive Health Education. The practical must be closely aligned with the theoretical education. In other words, one must be willing to make lifestyle changes or behavioral modification. In essence, my friend, this is similar to your accepting Jesus Christ as your Savior because both require lifestyle changes or behavioral modification. Diet control takes the power of God to be successful!

An Old Testament scripture appropriate for this component of the ministry is found in Deuteronomy 14:3- 23 This reveals the harmful nature of many foods (e.g. red meat) that we eat today-though they taste good! Barbecued ribs are an important example.

To further emphasize the effectiveness of diet control requires the same type of mind-set that is required when a sinner answers the call to come to Jesus Christ. He/she agrees to turn away from things in the past, which demand lifestyle changes or behavior modification. To make our bodies better to do the work of the kingdom, we must turn away from things of the past (e.g. eating harmful foods) and know that your "bodies are the temple of the Holy Spirit." Eat well and healthily.

> Eat more fresh fruit (5-6 times a day).
> Eat no fatty foods.
> Eat no fried foods.
> Do not drink alcoholic beverages.

A nutritionist or dietitian can be brought in to explain the proper diet to the members of the ministry specifically and the congregation in general.

Scriptural Meditations for Diet Control

> *"Thou shalt not eat any abominable thing."* Deuteronomy 14:3 KJV

> *"And the swine . it is unclean unto you. Ye shall not eat of their flesh nor touch their dead carcasses."*
> Deuteronomy 14:8 KJV

> *"These ye shall eat of, all that are in the water; all that have fins and scales shall ye eat."*
> Deuteronomy 14:9 KJV

> "And whatsoever hath not fins and scales, ye may not eat; it is unclean unto you"
> Deuteronomy 14:10 KJV

> "Do not destroy the work of God for the sake of food. All things indeed are pure, but it is evil for the man/woman who eats with offense." Romans 14:20 KJV

It is true that our bodies make up the temples of the Holy Spirit, therefore we should not desecrate them through the eating of unhealthy foods. Exercise and diet control are necessary to help in the prevention of cancer and heart disease-the number one killer! One-third of all cancer deaths are diet related.

PERIODIC HEALTH SCREENINGS

These cover the spectrum-cancers (prostate, breast, colon), STDs (sexually transmitted diseases), mental health and immunizations. These must be done on a periodic basis by men, women, boys and girls as applicable. Guidelines have been established for the screenings. Literature is available through the Health Department and other related agencies. In some case the screenings can be conducted on the church premises. Physicians from the community may be solicited for the screenings. The significance of the screenings lies in the fact that they can be life saving if acted upon expeditiously.

Remember the telephone numbers to your local Health Department, hospitals, and other health agencies because they want to become involved in the community.

Scriptural Meditations for Periodic Health Screenings

> "Now unto Him that is able to keep you from falling."
> Jude 24 KJV

> "Beloved, I wish above all things that thou mayest prosper and be in good health even as thy soul prospereth."
> The Third Epistle of John 2 KJV

"Know ye not that your body is the temple of the Holy Spirit."
1 Corinthians 6:19 KJV

PERIODIC HEALTH SCREENINGS (types)

Cancer screenings (Prostate, Breast, Colon, Cervix).

Sexually transmitted diseases (STD).

Mental Health (Depression).

Immunizations-aid greatly in preventive health.

Do the screenings on a periodic basis, for men, women, boys and girls when applicable. Guidelines have been established by the American Cancer Society. You may call them for specific literature at 1-800-ACS-2345.

In some cases, the screenings can be conducted on church premises.

Volunteers-recruit prayerfully and vigorously.

There are many other screenings which can be done; they are left to your discretion.

THE CHRISTIAN HEALTH LECTURE SERIES

What do these lectures do?
These lectures afford the church family and the underserved inhabitants of the inner city community the opportunity to become educated regarding preventive health matters.

Where are they held?
The lectures are usually held at the church.

What is the subject matter?
The subject matter of the lectures should be varied and the presentation should be in simple everyday language. The subject matter must be relevant.

What is the impact?
The impact of this component should serve as the catalyst to increase our level of consciousness regarding Preventive Health Education Awareness.

Who are the speakers?
They are individuals (physicians, osteopaths, nurses, medical technicians, chiropractors, etcetera) from the local community. Your personal physician may wish to participate.

What about scheduling and timing of the lectures?
This is critically important because you want to reach the most people and increase their Preventive Health Education Awareness relative to their "bodies, the temples of the Holy Spirit."

How are these lectures publicized?
The public knowledge of the times that the lectures will be held is vitally important for this aspect of the community outreach to be effective. It is to be understood that the lecture times will be announced appropriately at the church services. The other announcements can be made through the print media's monthly or quarterly publications.

The print media (newspapers, monthly or quarterly publications).

Flyers.

Electronic Media-public service announcements.

Word-of-mouth.

Any other method which you may choose to use.

Remember that with deep cutbacks in health care and related programs, these lectures are most important to us! The range of topics and subject matter that can be used is unlimited.

Scriptural Meditations for The Christian Health Lecture Series

> *"Study to show thyself approved unto God, a workman (woman) that needeth not to be ashamed, rightly dividing the word of truth."*
> 2 Timothy 2:15 KJV

> *"Beloved, I wish above all things that thou mayest prosper and be in good health even as thy soul prospereth."*
> 1 John: 1:2 KJV

SUPPORT GROUPS

> *"Cast thy burdens upon the Lord and He shall sustain thee; He shall never suffer the righteous to be moved"*
> Psalms 55:22

> *"Bear ye one another's burden and so fulfill the law of Christ"*
> Galatians 6:2

There is an urgent need for Support Groups in the Household of Faith.

Implicit in the above scriptures is the Divine Mandate from the Master for us to come together supporting one another in sickness and health.

We have multiple diseases, knowingly and unknowingly that are besetting and besieging us in our congregations, constantly, therefore it's most imperative that we come together in Support Groups for specific disease entities. This aids us tremendously in effecting better health and disease understanding, for the saints, so as to bring about more disease free and effective workers in the vineyard of God.

A Support Group can be formed for any disease entity.

Some of the Support Groups in equipping the saints are:

1. **Breast Cancer Support Group**
2. **Prostate Cancer Support Group**
3. **Colon Cancer Support Group**
4. **General Cancer Support Group** (this group is inclusive for all of the cancer groups) Assistance is available from your local American Cancer Society.
5. **Diabetes Support Group** (assistance is available from your local American Diabetes Association)
6. **Hypertension** (high blood pressure) **Support Group** (assistance is available from your local American Heart Association)
7. **Nutrition** (diet) **Support Group** (assistance is available from your local Health Department)
8. **Obesity** (overweight) **Support Group** (assistance is available from your church)
9. **Grief Support Group** (assistance is available from your church)
10. **Kidney Support Group** (assistance is available from your local American Kidney Foundation)

Your church can organize Support Groups to be consistent with your congregation. Some of these may be Arthritis, AIDS, etc.

Chapter Four

Water

Essential to Maintaining Good Health

The Bible speaks to the critically essential nature of water as spoken by the words of the Master, Jesus Christ, Himself.

> *"If any man/woman thirst, let him/her come unto me and drink"* John 7:37

> *"He/she that believeth on me as the scripture hath said, out of his/her heart shall flow rivers of living water"* John 7:38

> *"For I will pour water upon him/her that is thirsty"* Isaiah 44:3

> *"Ho, everyone that thirsteth come to the water"* Isaiah 55:1

Without water we die

Water constitutes between 50 and 70 percent of total body weight. The average normal value for young adult males is 60 percent of body weight and 50 percent for young adult females. Since fat contains little water, the lean individual has a greater proportion of water to total body weight than the obese (fat) person. The lower the percentage of total body water in females is due to the large amount of fatty tissue and small muscle mass. Total body water decreases steadily and significantly with age.

The majority of the earth's surface, e.g. rivers, lakes, oceans, etc. is composed of water.

It is an understatement to say that water is an essential ingredient of good health. Every person should recognize that water plays a tremendously great role in his/her health daily. For example, one of the health implications of water is that it is essential in "flushing the kidneys" in the elimination of toxic substances from the body daily. Adequate hydration of the body depends upon you and your views regarding water.

A simple, easy to follow schedule for drinking the proverbial eight glasses of water daily is this:

Drink:
1. 1 8 oz. glass of water - upon rising
2. 1 8 oz. glass of water - with breakfast
3. 1 8 oz. glass of water - between breakfast and lunch
4. 1 8 oz. glass of water - with lunch
5. 1 8 oz. glass of water - after lunch
6. 1 8 oz. glass of water - with supper (dinner)
7. 1 8 oz. glass of water - after supper
8. 1 8 oz. glass of water - at bedtime
8 glasses of water!

This is a schedule (routine), you may want to develop your own-which is best for you.

Many people do not eat breakfast but remember that water is essential to your good health. Take charge of your health with lifestyle changes and behavioral modification.

Preventive health education is the key.

Chapter Five

Planning the Community Health Fair

The **Annual Health Fair** at the Local Church

This health fair is more amenable and easily carried out on the local church grounds. It is the one that serves the local congregation and its immediate surrounding community, which is invited.

Without question, this health fair at the local church is the highly recommended one for the individual church, at least on an annual basis. It could also be called **The Annual Health Awareness Day or The Annual Health Seminar**, etc.

The components of the annual Health Fair at the local church are:

1. The General Chairperson or Coordinator.

Duties: the overall responsibility of various committees which are charged with the bringing together of the participants in the health fair. This person is extremely critical to the overall success of the fair. He/she must be dedicated and committed one hundred percent to the project. The best laid plans may sometimes go astray; therefore it is essential to keep the Pastor appraised from the beginning of the project. This cannot be overemphasized!

To call and conduct meetings of the committees which are:

1. Program and Participants
2. Publicity and Entertainment
3. Security and Clean-up
4. Funding and Budget
5. Food and Vendors
6. Children's Activities
7. Seminar e.g. health lectures
(demonstrations)

The meetings of the Health Fair Committee at the local church should start at least four to six months before the date of the fair. This is crucial to the smooth operation of the fair itself.

Brief explanation of the various committees:

1. Program and Participants

This committee is charged with the responsibility of arranging the program with its participants to include such things as:

Cancer screenings and information lectures (e.g. prostate and breast)

Dangers of smoking tobacco

Exercise

Diet and Nutrition

Blood Pressure Control

Diabetes

Living with Arthritis

Teenage Pregnancy

STDs (Sexually Transmitted Diseases)

This a partial sample of a very exhaustive list. Do not forget to call upon your local health departments and other health resources for help with this project.

2. Publicity and Entertainment

It is very important to get the message out to the congregation such as in the church bulletin board and announcements, PSA (Public Service Announcements) via print and electronic media. Entertainment can include gospel singing, step shows, high school bands, etcetera. This is flexible according to what is available to you. Include entertainment for children such as in the Bounce House, Face Painting, etcetera. This is also included under the committee for children's activities.

3. Security and Clean-up

This committee is to be responsible for the overall security of the seminar and fair area and the general clean-up of the area after the seminar/fair is over. The importance of this committee is truly vital to the smooth operation of the event.

Note: There may be those in the congregation that have experience in this area of expertise. Do not fail to survey the membership for those who may be able to assist in this committee. This holds true for all other committees as well.

4. Funding and Budget

The funding can come from the Health Ministry budget, if there is one available, at the church. If one is not available, then other avenues of funding must be pursued. A partial list of funding sources follows:

Health care entities/organizations-HMOs, insurance companies, etcetera.

Personal donations/contributions-The budget will, of necessity, be proposed according to the scope of activities or components of the seminar/fair. You should remember that many of the services and products can be donated. An example of this is that the printing of the flyers can be done free of charge by a printing company.

5. Food and Vendors

The food may be donated, in part, by food chains. You must start early with your solicitation of these organizations because there are many chains of command which must be gone through for approval.

Though they are not healthy, hot dogs are very popular at health seminars/fairs. You should strive to have healthy foods-fruits, healthy drinks-available.

The vendors are unlimited. They include:

Chiropractic demonstrations
Massage (ethical) demonstrations
Health service organizations such as Hospice, American Cancer Society, American Heart Association, etcetera.

The charge, if any, for the vendors should be minimal. It is doubtful, for instance, that a volunteer-operated nonprofit organization such as The American Cancer Society should be asked to donate financially.

6. Children's Activities

Theses activities should be planned so as to keep the children busy in a wholesome and healthful way. As stated previously, under Publicity and Entertainment, The Bounce House and Face Painting are very popular with children. A fire truck is another thing that is very popular. You may be innovative in this regard.

7. Seminars and Health Lectures

These seminars are the key to the Health Fair's success and thought should enter into the planning of the participants. Examples of seminar participants are:

Blood Pressure Lecture and Screening
Since many African Americans suffer disproportionately from this disease of hypertension, otherwise known as high blood pressure, and its complications that follow, such as strokes, kidney failure, it should have top priority on the list.

Sexually Transmitted Diseases (STDs)
HIV/AIDS is contributing to kill and devastate our communities, therefore its inclusion for presentation in a professional, ethical and Christian way should be done.

Cancer Screenings
These include screening for prostate cancer, "killer of black men." We have the highest incident and mortality rate (death) of any group in the world. To have our men checked early for this treatable disease is of the utmost importance. The women can play a vital role in getting the men out to be checked. Other cancers that can be screened are:

Breast Cancer (mammograms)
Cervical Cancer (pap smears)
Colon Cancer (hemocult of the stool)

The above list, with explanations, is specifically geared to the Annual Health Fair at the local Church. Its success requires organization, planning and dedication on the part of unselfish volunteers. The next project that can be done is:

The Annual Community Health Fair (Community Health Outreach)

The most important thing to remember about a Health Fair which is beyond the immediate grounds of the church is that it is a major, major undertaking. You must not embark on this monumental task without proper planning and dedicated volunteers. A prudent suggestion is that you start with the health fair on your local church grounds. This is suggested so as to get you acclimated or accustomed to the larger Community Health Fair.

A list of the Annual Health Fair Components follows:

1. **Health Screenings for Cancer**
   Prostate - PSA (Prostate Specific Antigen), blood test and digital rectal exam
   Breast - screening mammograms
   Cervix - pap smears
   Colon - Hemmocult Stool Test for blood

2. **Other Health Screenings**
   Cholesterol (high fat in the blood)
   Diabetes (sugar)
   Glaucoma (eye)
   Sickle cell anemia
   Osteoporosis (soft bones), if available
   Asthma
   Dental (if available)
   Body fat measurement

3. **Mental Health**

4. **STD** (Sexually Transmitted Diseases)

5. **Health Literature:** This literature includes a wide range of health topics and diseases relevant to the African American community, e.g. cancer, diabetes, hypertension (high blood pressure), high cholesterol, HIV/AIDS, dangers of smoking tobacco,

etcetera. Exercise and diet are also included.

Health Maintenance Organization (HMOs)-These groups are amenable to participating in the health fairs because preventive health education. Childhood Immunizations: Call upon your local health department to assist you in this very important segment of the fair.

7. **Major health-related organizations to be asked to participate are:**

The American Cancer Society-This organization fosters programs in prevention, early detection, education and advocacy for cancer control and treatment.

The American Lung Association-Has a long history in the fight against the harmful effects of smoking tobacco, e.g. lung cancer, emphysema, and other lung diseases.

The American Heart Association-With its expertise in heart disease lends much to increase the preventive education relative to heart disease.

The Mental Health Association-Is able to do mental health screenings at the fair. These are important to our mental health and wellness. Some cities have a Black Psychologist Association and it should be solicited to participate, if one is available. Remember that mental depression is prevalent in the African American community.

The American Diabetes Association-Helps to give information regarding diabetic health information is important to them and their programs of good health. They should be approached to participate in the health fair.

Local Hospitals

Human Services

Medical Suppliers

County Medical Associations

African American Medical Societies-e.g. Dr. James Sistrunk Medical Society in Ft. Lauderdale/Broward County

Black Nurses Association

Dental Association (African American)

Civic Organizations-e;g; Urban League, National Association for the Advancement of Colored People, Homeowners Associations, Chambers of Commerce, etcetera.

Chapter Six

Summary and Conclusions
Summary:

This Health and Wellness Ministry Model expands upon the previous Health Ministry at Mount Bethel Baptist Church, Fort Lauderdale, Florida. It was called the Health and Welfare Ministry. The word "welfare" is deleted because of its negative connotation by members in the African American community.

Most people are aware of their health though they may not be able to understand the multiplicity of diseases that affect their bodies. This was very evident during the training sessions presented. The author's medical degree, ordination as a Baptist Minister and his theological education give him a uniquely appreciated perspective on the Health Ministry.

An important person to be dealt with seriously is the Church Pastor who is the ex officio member of the Health and Wellness Ministry of the local congregation. He/she must be given his/her respect, especially in this ministry. Further, most Pastors are busy, therefore, for a Health Ministry to be accepted, the author believes that its outline must be easily understood and implemented. As a consequence of that stance, all superfluous ingredients are removed from the core of the ministry.

The author cannot overemphasize the significance of the

Pastor's role in this Ministry. This is true of other church ministries as well. Everyone (Ministry and Church Pastor) should be on the "same page," e.g. thinking the same way, relative to the ministry and its functions. In view of the fact that the Health and Wellness Ministry is relatively new, on a practical level, its position must be understood. The Ministry is young, compared to some others, e.g. missionary ministry. Because of this there is a tremendous amount of prayer, dedicated teaching/training (Biblically founded) needed to foster a vibrant and beneficial ministry for the congregation.

Having done that, this author sincerely believes it to be prudent to present a **Model-in-Ministry** that is acceptable and adaptable by churches (pastors) in general.

The author marvels at the enthusiasm of those participants at the sessions. Questions of importance are raised. Probably the greatest compliment that he remembers receiving (from participants) was that "I did not know" pertinent scriptures in the beginning but "Now I do know!" Statements like these had untold depths of meaning to him personally. It is to be understood, unequivocally, that this Preventive Health Education is most notably effective when there are concomitant lifestyle changes. This is very crucial. Those lifestyle changes truly separate those who hear the health message and fail to act upon it from those who hear it and act, effectuating lifestyle changes for the better. The measurement of the lifestyle changes is in the form of statements (e.g. "I now give more attention to my diet.") made by participants. This is evident by better nutritional habits and exercise. The basic goal is for everyone to take charge of his/her health.

The previous ministry was basically composed of a Minister of Health and Wellness ("Welfare") and volunteers.

The Christian Health lecture series contributes to the greatest number of programs for the congregation and the community.

Those lectures include pertinent topics, e.g. hypertension (high blood pressure), arthritis, heart disease and cancer, among others. The lecturers are prominent African American health care providers on the local and national levels.

Periodic blood pressure screenings are also conducted. Small

Health Fairs are held at the Church. They are beneficial but the attendance is lower than anticipated. This could be remedied by more effective advertising and promotion of the event. Obviously, improvement in this area would be welcomed. These mini-health fairs could be conducted at the Church as often as the Ministry would deem necessary.

The Annual Community Health Fair (Community Health Outreach) does not preclude Churches from holding their own health fairs. It is important to clearly understand this concept.

The Annual Community Health Fair is held in conjunction with other churches ("interfaith linkages"), the local Department of Health and other agencies providing health care. The interfaith linkages prove the positive value of churches working together for the common good of humankind.

This physician's expertise gives ample credibility to his position as Minister of Health and Wellness.

Historically speaking it could be stated that the closest thing to a Health Ministry is the Nurse's Guild.

African Americans are generally less informed than other ethnic groups (e.g Hispanics) in society. Being less informed, from an educational perspective, contributes to their not adhering to Preventive Health Education.

Tradition (perpetuation of the status quo) keeps us away from the mainstream regarding health care.

Economically, it goes without saying that African Americans are shut out of the mainstream relative to affordable health care.

From the practical perspective it is said that the information herein, dating back to Genesis, allows the utilization of those principles even to this day, e.g., Genesis 3 KJV and Deuteronomy, Chapter 14, KJV.

In continued movement toward the resolution of the problem previously identified, the author designs a Model-in-Ministry which can be implemented in the African American church.

The basic design of the model consists of three major parts. In recapitulation they are:

1. **The Minister of Health and Wellness**
2. **Preventive Health Education**
3. **Community Health Outreach**

The basic structure above allows for easy understanding and application (implementation) of the model.

Conclusions:

The author diminishes the lack of Preventive Health Education through an effective Health and Wellness Ministry at Mount Bethel Baptist Church.

The above is accomplished by the design and implementation of a three component model which is replicable.

The Health Academy and Health Disciples are new and innovative.

The major effort of Community Health Outreach is accomplished by the Annual Community Health Fair.

In recapitulation, the author states that there existed the Problem: lack of Preventive Health Education and need for an effective Health and Wellness Ministry in the African American Church. It is treated with intensive training sessions (the Bible Study Groups and the Health Academy and Health Disciples). The Results yield increased Preventive Health Education Awareness also an effective Health and Wellness Ministry!

Chapter Seven

Course Outlines
The Health And Wellness Ministry
In The African American Church
Preventive Health Education

COURSE OUTLINE

Place: Any Church, USA

Session One (1-1/2 hours)
Opening Prayer
Introduction to the Ministry (Course)
Purpose of Pre-test and Post-test (Questionnaires)
Administer Pre-test (Questionnaire)
Course Objectives
Brief history of the Ministry
Nurses Guild
Genesis 43:27 and 28
1 Corinthians 6:19: ."*.. your body is the temple of the Holy Spirit."*
Begin with Minister of Health and Wellness
Corps of Volunteers (who they are and their functions)
Laity Training

Interactive question and answer period
Closing Prayer

Session Two (1-1/2 Hours)
Opening Prayer
Results of Pre-test (Questionnaire)
Brief review of Session One, Preventive Health Education-Awareness
Continuation of Ministry's Components
Preventive Health Education-Awareness
Exercise and Diet Control
Christian Health Lecture Series
Interactive Question and Answer Period
Closing Prayer

Session Three (1-1/2 hours)
Opening Prayer
Brief review of Session Two
Continuation of Ministry's components
Holistic (Body, Romans 12:1; Mind, 2 Timothy 1:7; Spirit, Romans 8:9)
Linkages with local Health Departments
Periodic Health Screenings (e.g. Prostate Cancer, Blood Pressure, etc.)
Interactive Question and Answer Period
Closing Prayer

Session Four (1-1/2 hours)
Opening Prayer
Brief review of Sessions One, Two and Three
Continuation of the Ministry's components
Health Academy (Health Disciples-youth)
Community Health Outreach - Annual Community Health Fair
Review of previous sessions
Interactive Question and Answer Period
Administer Post-test (Questionnaire)
Test evaluation
Closing Prayer

THE HEALTH AND WELLNESS MINISTRY IN THE AFRICAN AMERICAN CHURCH PREVENTIVE HEALTH EDUCATION
INTRODUCTION TO THE MINISTRY
Session One (1-1/2 hours)

COURSE OUTLINE

Place: Any Church, USA

Opening Prayer
Introduction to the Ministry (Course)
Purpose of Pre-test and Post-test (Questionnaires)
Administer Pre-test (Questionnaire)
Course Objectives
Brief history of the Ministry
Nurses Guild
Genesis 43:27 and 28
1 Corinthians 6:19: ."*.. your body is the temple of the Holy Spirit.*"
Begin with Minister of Health and Wellness
Corps of Volunteers (who they are and their functions)
Laity Training
Interactive question and answer period
Closing Prayer

INTRODUCTION

THE PROBLEM

The basic problem that this model-in-ministry concentrates on is two-fold:

1. The lack of Preventive Health Education Awareness in the African American Church.

2. A need for an effective Health and Welfare Ministry (in the

African American Church) through which the basic lack of Preventive Health Education Awareness can be diminished.

THE PROJECT FOCUS

The project focus is to provide a replicable model-in-ministry which enables the participants to acquire basic Preventive Health Education and increase their levels of health awareness.

This model-in-ministry expands upon the existing Health and Wellness Ministry at Mount Bethel Baptist Church.

OBJECTIVES

1. To effectively increase Preventive Health Education Awareness in the African American Church.

2. To establish a Health and Wellness Ministry Model which should effectively increase Preventive Health Education Awareness in the African American Church.

3. To teach some essentials of Biblically founded Preventive Health Education Awareness (e.g. *"The body is the temple of the Holy Spirit."* 1 Corinthians 6:19)

4. To introduce important health information relative to Prostate Cancer Screenings, as an example, of a tool, to help diminish this disease; its disproportionately devastating incidence and mortality in the African American male population.

5. To teach our youth, in the Health Academy, some important Biblical principles of Preventive Health Education Awareness (e.g. healthy lifestyles).

6. To introduce program participants to (the design, implemen-

tation and evaluation of a replicable Health and Wellness Ministry Model) which includes information relative to a Community Health Fair, for Community Health Outreach.

THE PROJECT DESIGN

This project is designed with the Basic Health and Wellness Ministry Structure which consists of 11 components. They are:

1. **Minister of Health and Wellness**
2. **Corps of Volunteers**
3. **Preventive Health Education**
4. **Exercise and Diet Control**
5. **Christian Health Lecture Series**
6. **Holistic (Body-Mind-Spirit)**
7. **Linkages with local Health Departments (& the Interfaith Community)**
8. **Periodic Health Screenings**
9. **Health Academy - Health Disciples (youth)**
10. **Laity Training**
11. **Community Health Outreach - Annual Community Health Fair**

The Minister of Health and Wellness may be either a Medical Doctor, Chiropractic Physician, Osteopathic Physician, Dentist, Registered Nurse, Licensed Practical Nurse, Medical Assistant, Medical Technician, Nurses Aide, a paramedical person or any lay person.

The Preventive Health Education is that which emanates from the teaching session of the ministry on an ongoing basis.

The Christian Health Lecture Series provides pertinent lectures by health care professionals and other health care-related personnel.

The Holistic (Body-Mind-Spirit) component involves the ministry's teachings to include the whole person.

The Linkages with local Health Departments is a very critical association for the Health Ministry to be effective. Their resources and personnel are there to help. Remember that they are tax-supported and **we pay taxes**.

The Periodic Health Screenings are ongoing and play a vital role in disease detection before it becomes serious and life threatening (e.g. Sickle-Cell Anemia, Prostate Cancer, Breast Cancer).

The Health Academy with Health Disciples consists of children ages 5 through 16 years.

The Laity Training is an ongoing process where individuals are trained to train others.

> "Study to show thyself approved unto God, a workman that needeth not to be ashamed rightly dividing the word of truth."
> 2 Timothy 2:15

The (Annual) Community Health Fair is an important Community Health Outreach Program. This provides an opportunity to reach out to the community and help increase its level of "health awareness." Local Health Departments can play a vital role in the Health Fair.

MINISTRY IMPLEMENTATION

Four one and one-half hour training sessions are held. These are geared to the diminishing of the lack of Preventive Health Education Awareness in the Church. All components are covered.

MINISTRY EVALUATION

A pre-test (Questionnaire) consistent with the Ministry's objectives is administered before the training sessions are taught. The same test is given after the training sessions are taught. This is to assess the increase in the effectiveness of Health Awareness relative to Preventive Health Education through the Health and Wellness Ministry. Additionally, an interactive question and answer period is allowed after each training session.

Purpose of Pre-test and Post-test (Questionnaires)

To assess the increase in the effectiveness of health awareness relative to preventive health education through the Health and Wellness Ministry.

Course Objectives

Brief History of the Ministry - Nurses Guild

Historically, the closest thing to a Health Ministry in the African American Church was (is) the traditional Nurses Guild, consisting of those who were not necessarily nurses at all. Qualifications - Expressed desire to serve, trained (RNs, LPNs, Aides) or untrained (e.g. make beds in hospital). "Desire to be" - more important than training. The Guild is always under the direct control of the Pastor.

Uniforms - White nurses uniforms; heavily starched.

Equipment - Church hand fan and bottle of smelling salt (an aromatic preparation used as a stimulant and restorative to relieve faintness).

Nurses - Stationed strategically around the pews, poised for action, e.g. "Shouting," uncontrolled body movements associated with varying sounds of different decibels. This provoked the responses of the nurses. Those members more prone to shout, were known. Blood pressure checks were unknown. There were no health related outreach programs.

The foregone descriptions were the extent of the traditional Nurses' Guild in the African American Church, to the writer's best recollection.

THE HEALTH AND WELLNESS MINISTRY IN THE AFRICAN AMERICAN CHURCH PREVENTIVE HEALTH EDUCATION
Session Two (1-1/2 Hours)

Place: Any Church, USA

Opening Prayer
Results of Pre-test (Questionnaire)
Brief review of Session One
Continuation of Ministry's Components
Preventive Health Education-Awareness
Exercise and Diet Control
Christian Health Lecture Series
Interactive Question and Answer Period
Closing Prayer

PREVENTIVE HEALTH EDUCATION-AWARENESS

1. This is a critically important core of the ministry.

2. It has been stated from time immemorial that *"an ounce of prevention is worth a pound of cure."*

3. Alfred Marshall (Economist) stated that *"We should think of the health of our community rather than the wealth of our community."*

4. The educational thrust is the broad instruction relative to the overall health education awareness of you - all church members and others in the community.

5. Less than one percent of the greater than one billion dollar health care budget is spent on preventive health education.

6. Most of the money spent on health care is spent on curative

measures (after the diseases have damaged our bodies).

7. For example, prenatal care (education) costs $1,500-$2,000 contrasted to no prenatal care (education) and a low birth weight (premature) infant for a cost of greater than $10,000.

8. The level of consciousness relative to preventive health education awareness must be significantly increased in our church and community (Remember 1 Corinthians 6:19, *"Your body is the temple of the Holy Spirit."*).

9. Read Jude 24, *"Now unto Him that is able to keep you from falling,"* speaks to us in the Health Ministry in regards to prevention in health education.

10. **Preventive Health Education-Awareness is the common thread of this ministry.**

EXERCISE AND DIET CONTROL

1. The objective here is to foster the assimilation of usable knowledge to members of the congregation (and the Community at large) regarding the value of Exercise and Diet Control.

2. Simple exercises, e.g. three times weekly on a regular basis can help to promote body strength, increase muscle tone and engender a sense of well-being.

3. Those with medical problems must consult their physicians before engaging in exercises.

4. Diet control and nutrition are extremely important in the maintaining of optimum health. It is well established in medical circles that control of one's blood pressure, regular exercise and not eating fatty foods can help in the prevention

of heart disease.

THE CHRISTIAN HEALTH LECTURE SERIES

1. This is an important vehicle to reach the under served inhabitants in the inner-city community.

2. A list of past and future speakers should be listed in the Speakers Bureau.

3. This component should enable the wider dissemination to the local community, in general.

4. The impact of this component should serve as a catalyst to increase our level of consciousness regarding Preventive Health Education Awareness.

5. Historically, we presented former Surgeon General Joycelyn Elders (Taking Charge of Your Health); LaSalle D. Leffall, Jr., M.D. (Former Professor of Surgery - Howard University College of Medicine), Breast Cancer - All You Need to Know; Freda Lewis Hall, M.D., noted psychiatrist spoke on "Depression in the African American Community," on Health Sunday, October 20, 1997, after the Health Fair.

6. Speakers on the local level are used also, e.g. Pamela Hall, Doctor of Psychology, "Stress Management," Edwina Hamilton-Bell, Doctor of Psychology, "Stress Management in the Black Community."

7. Scheduling and timing of the lectures are of the utmost importance.

8. All topics must be relevant.

9. With deep cutbacks in health care and related programs,

these lectures are most important to us.

10. Public dissemination of lecture times is vitally important for community outreach to be effective.

THE HEALTH AND WELLNESS MINISTRY IN THE AFRICAN AMERICAN CHURCH PREVENTIVE HEALTH EDUCATION PERIODIC HEALTH SCREENINGS
(Session Three (1-1/2 hours)

Place: Any Church, USA

Opening Prayer
Brief review of Session Two
Continuation of Ministry's components
Holistic (Body, Romans 12:1; Mind, 2 Timothy. 1:7; Spirit, Romans 8:9)
Linkages with local Health Departments
Periodic Health Screenings (e.g. Prostate Cancer, Blood Pressure, etc.)
Interactive Question and Answer Period
Closing Prayer

THE HOLISTIC COMPONENT
BODY-MIND-SPIRIT

This Holistic approach is fully utilized and is of primary importance. It is of significance especially relative to the Preventive Health Education in this ministry. The total concept of God's temple (your body) is critical to the understanding of this component of the ministry.

> THE BODY - *"I beseech you therefore, brethren by the mercies of God, that you present your bodies a living sacrifice, holy, acceptable unto God, which is your reasonable service."*

Romans 12:1

THE MIND - *"For God hath not given us the spirit of fear, but of power, and of love, and of a sound mind."*
2 Timothy 1:9

THE SPIRIT - *"But ye are not in the flesh but in the Spirit, if so be that the Spirit of God dwell in you. Now if any man/woman have not the Spirit of Christ he/she is none of His."*
Romans 8:9

THE CHURCH HEALTH MINISTRY

Linkages with local Health Departments

This should ensure that the largest number of citizens benefit from **preventive health education awareness**.

"And we know that all things work together for good to them that love God, to them who are the called according to His purpose."
Romans 8:28

Linkages with Local Health Departments and the Inter-Faith Community

The solicitation of support from the tax-supported health departments and hospitals is essential.

Remember that we pay the taxes for the operation of these departments and hospitals. They are there to help us reduce those diseases which are preventable. This is in line with our basic goal in **Preventive Health Education Awareness**. The support is there for the asking!

Health issues should bridge the gap of scriptural and theological interpretive minutiae or the splitting of the proverbial theological hairs. It is an established fact that diseases, and their consequences are transdenominational. This means that diseases affect and inflict us in a non-discriminatory way, without regard to time, place, age, sex or religious beliefs.

PERIODIC HEALTH SCREENINGS

These include the spectrum of those diseases which can be cured when detected early. As has been stated in this document, there are many diseases which devastate our communities like no other group in the United States. For example, Prostate Cancer kills more Black men that any other group in the world!

Studies, however, have shown that there is a 90% plus cure rate if the disease is detected and treated earlywhile it's still in the capsule of the gland. African American women with Breast Cancer survive for shorter time periods than White women. Blood pressure screenings were done among others.

These screenings are focused on detecting disease states before they became deleteriously devastating and beyond cure.

The screenings are done on the church premises when appropriate and at other times at local health care facilities (e.g. hospitals, clinics). There are many health screenings, to name a few - mammograms for breast cancer, PSA blood test (Prostate Specific Antigen) for prostate cancer, Hemmocult Stool Test (occult blood in the stool for colorectal cancer), mental health screenings, asthma screenings and STD (sexually transmitted diseases) to name a few.

As has been stated in the objectives: #4 "to introduce important health information relative to Prostate Cancer Screening, as an example, of a tool, to help eradicate this disease, its disproportionately devastating incidence and mortality in the African American male population."

Some facts about Prostate Cancer in African American Men

1. Prostate Cancer is the most common male cancer in the

United States.

2. Though this cancer is prevalent among men in general, African Americans suffer disproportionately relative to its occurrence and mortality.

3. African Americans have the highest incidence and mortality of prostate cancer in the world.

4. African Americans have more than twice the mortality rate compared to members of the majority community.

5. Prostate Cancer is usually a slow growing malignancy; like most cancers it can be cured if diagnosed and treated early. Early Detection is the key.

6. The basic screening blood test is the PSA (Prostate Specific Antigen). This test must be done in conjunction with the DRE (Digital Rectal Exam) by a physician.

7. The acute level of public awareness relative to prostate cancer is below what it should be as compared to that of breast cancer.

8. There are formidable obstacles which must be overcome relative to prostate cancer screening.

Some of the more important obstacles and opportunities are:

1. The African American church - pillar of the community, e.g. haven for the depressed and poverty stricken and shelter in the time of storm.

2. Fear and distrust of the medical establishment, e.g. Tuskegee experiment.

3. Fear of losing their testicles e.g. thinking that impotence will occur if they get prostate cancer.

4. Involvement of females in the recruitment (screening) process.

5. Utilization of the team approach e.g. those of like ethnic backgrounds.

6. Strong educational programs in partnership with the American Cancer Society should help to address the high incidence in African American men.

The above factors and obstacles should be significantly reduced through the efforts of the Health and Wellness Ministry and Preventive Health Education Awareness in the African American Church.

THE HEALTH AND WELLNESS MINISTRY IN THE AFRICAN AMERICAN CHURCH PREVENTIVE HEALTH EDUCATION

THE HEALTH ACADEMY HEALTH DISCIPLES (YOUTH) ANNUAL COMMUNITY HEALTH FAIR (COMMUNITY HEALTH OUTREACH)
Session Four (1-1/2 hours)

Place: Any Church, USA

Opening Prayer
Brief review of Sessions One, Two and Three
Continuation of the Ministry's components
Health Academy (Health Disciples-youth)
Annual Community Health Fair (Community Health Outreach)
Review of previous sessions
Interactive Question and Answer Period
Administer Post-test (Questionnaire)
Test evaluation
Closing Prayer

THE HEALTH ACADEMY
Its Need - Purpose - Composition - Implementation

THE NEED - There is an urgently dire need for children, in their formative years, to know the general nature of preventive health education measures and the things that should be done to prevent many diseases. The need is clear in regards to early **Preventive Health Education** so as to decrease chronic debilitating diseases in later years.

THE PURPOSE - The purpose of the Health Academy is to fulfill the need, as stated above, by teaching children the vital importance of maintaining healthy bodies. The teaching includes the value of proper exercising, dieting, the dangers of smoking (tobacco) and the essential nature of proper sex education (Biblically founded). They are taught the important points about ecology (the branch of biology that deals with the relations between living organisms and their environment) e.g. clean air and water.

The goal is to actively raise their conscious level of **Preventive Health Education Awareness** to unprecedented heights.

THE COMPOSITION - The Health Academy should be composed of young children from the ages of five years through high school. Members of this academy are called "Health Disciples."

THE IMPLEMENTATION - Through the active participation of the Health Disciples, there are structured teaching sessions on pertinent health topics, e.g. exercise, healthy diet, dangers of smoking, rewards of healthy lifestyles and the dangers of unhealthy lifestyles.

This is an extremely exciting program with the potential to help diminish the continuing ever-increasing spiral of devastating diseases and environmentally harmful conditions in the African American community. Biblical undergirdings for the significantly relevance of the Health Academy are as follows:

GENERAL THEME

> "Train up a child in the way he should go and when he is old, he will not depart from it."
> Proverbs 22:6

> "And ye fathers provoke not your children unto wrath, but bring them up in the nurture and admonition of the Lord."
> Ephesians 6:4

"Lo children are an heritage from the Lord." Psalm 127:3

VALUABLE SCRIPTURES FOR SEX EDUCATION

"But fornication, and all uncleanness, or covetousness, let it not be once named among you, as becometh saints."
Ephesians 5:3

"For this we know that no fornicator, nor unclean person, nor covetous man (who is an idolater) hath any inheritance in the kingdom of Christ and of God."
Ephesians 5:5

VALUABLE SCRIPTURE FOR SESSIONS ON CONDUCT

"Neither filthiness nor foolish talking nor jesting, which are not convenient (fitting), but rather, giving of thanks."
Ephesians 5:4

THE ANNUAL COMMUNITY HEALTH FAIR
Community Health Outreach

This is an extremely important Community Health Outreach program. The major emphasis is on **Preventive Health Education Awareness**. Early detection (of disease) is the key ingredient.

Consequently, the Health Fair provides a golden opportunity to reach out into the community and help increase its level of **"Health Awareness."**

As with any major project of this magnitude commitment and proper planning are essential. It is to be understood that mini health fairs should be held, on-site, at the local churches. These are vital to the health and wellness of the congregations. These mini health fairs should be conducted periodically at the discretion of the local church.

The needs, purpose and composition of the Annual Community Health Fair - Community Health Outreach are:

THE NEED - Because of the skyrocketing costs of remedial health care, there isn't any doubt that a community-wide health fair should help to stifle and reduce the ever present high percentage of devastating diseases. Preventive health education awareness and health screenings should be addressed adequately at the health fair.

THE PURPOSE - To carry the message of preventive health education awareness and early detection of disease to the inner-city community (underserved, uninsured).

THE COMPOSITION - The Health Fair Task Force should be composed of the local Health and Wellness Ministry and invited churches in the community. The participants are not restricted to any denomination, sect or creed-all are welcomed to partake of this opportunity to help alleviate devastating diseases which do not discriminate on religious bases. The Health Fair Components are discussed in the following paragraphs.

Health Screenings for Cancer (prostate, breast and cervix), cholesterol, sickle cell anemia, glaucoma, mental health, dental. Health literature is distributed, childhood immunizations are given. Health Departments are very important and may provide needed assistance in the screenings.

The American Cancer Society plays a vital role in cancer prevention and the saving of lives. They may assist in underwriting the costs of mammograms, if funds are available.

The American Heart Association, with its expertise in heart disease, lends much to preventive education relative to heart disease.

The American Diabetes Association helps to provide information regarding diabetic health education.

The American Lung Association has a storied history of the fight against the harmful effects of smoking tobacco, lung cancer and other lung diseases. They are asked to participate.

The Mental Health Association is able to conduct mental health screenings at the fair. These are important to our mental health and wellness.

The Women in Distress, Human Services, HRS, local hospitals and other health care providers are invited to participate.

Asthma Screenings

Blood Pressure Screenings

Body Fat Measurements, if available.

Osteoporosis Screenings, if available.

Medical, civic, fraternal and professional organizations help make up the exhaustive list of potential participants.

THE IMPLEMENTATION is primarily through a Community Health Fair Task Force, the Health and Wellness Ministry of a local church, the Health Committee, The Nurses Guild, etcetera, and all local churches who are amenable to participating. Local church participation is essential to the health fair's success. The minister of Health and Wellness or the chairman of the health committee or the Nurses Guild may serve as the as general chairman or coordinator of the health fair.

Participation of the church pastors is highly desirable. They should be apprised of the fair through key members of their congregation, who will work on the task force. The date of the fair must be acceptable to all participating parties. The site is uniquely critical because a "neutral site" (one not on any church ground) should ensure greater community participation. This also allows for more flexibility. Suggested sites may be a local school or city park.

A list of task force committees is as follows:

1. Budget - essential to estimate costs early; many goods and services may be donated.
2. Children's activities - these allow for entertainment of the children.
3. Clean-up
4. Entertainment
5. Food
6. Funding
7. Hostesses
8. Participants
9. Program
10. Security
11. Publicity
12. Seminars (health lectures)
13. Vendors

Chapter Eight

Sermons

Two sermons delivered at the June 1997 Hampton University Ministers' Conference:

SERMON ONE
Your Body – Temple of the Holy Spirit
It's Creation – Cost – and Care
(Don't Desecrate the Temple)
"Know Ye Not That Your Body Is The Temple Of The Holy Spirit?"
I Corinthians 6:19

SERMON TWO
Is There A Doctor In The House?
*"And a woman having an issue of blood twelve years, who has spent all her living upon
physicians, neither could be healed by any."*
Luke 8:43
*"Came behind Him and touched the border of His garment; and immediately her issue of
blood stanched or stopped."*
Luke 8:44

SERMON ONE
Your Body – Temple of the Holy Spirit
Its Creation – Cost – and Care
(Don't Desecrate The Temple)

"Know Ye Not That Your Body Is The Temple Of The Holy Spirit?"
I Corinthians 6:19

Health is implicit in Holiness and Wholeness. Health is often defined as the absence of disease. A person may say in answer to the query, "How are you?" "I'm healthy, thank you. I haven't caught a cold all winter long." Someone else may say, "My stomach was upset for two weeks after I ate barbecued ribs and potato salad, but I'm healthy now."

The concepts or ideal states of Holiness and Wholeness usually are interpreted relative to time, place and person. Holiness may be one thing for a Baptist in Moscow, and another thing for a South African Episcopalian, or a Four-Square Pentecostal, or a Boston Christian Scientist.

Wholeness may be one thing for a Northern high school athlete, and another thing for a poverty-stricken Southern teenager, or a paraplegic who is the victim of a drive-by-shooting, or a Daytona Beach retiree.

God's will is always a demand to be holy in a given place and at a given time. Holiness should be holiness anywhere and anytime.

To obtain an understanding of experiencing God in Holiness and Wholeness we should see how He views our bodies. This can be accomplished by looking at a question posed by Paul in I Cor. 6:19 – *"Know Ye Not That Your Body Is The Temple Of The Holy Spirit?"*

Without optimal health we are deprived of that needed energy, so vitally necessary for the essential work in God's vineyard.

In today's life, we are primarily concerned about what brand to make our possessions – from our Timex to our Rolex, Piaget, Patek Phillipe watches; from our Stacy-Adams shoes to our Allen-Edmond shoes; from our cords of Schowbilt suits to our Hart Schaffner and Mark and our Brioni suits, shirts and ties; from Hugo Boss, Countess Mara and Stephanie Ricci; from our Yugos to our Lincolns, Cadillacs and Mercedes Benz automobiles, not only that but dresses, colognes and perfumes from Neiman-Marcus and Saks Fifth Avenue. Further, we live tucked away in our beautiful, three-tiered mansions in gated communities. Everyone wants to know who made it – what's the manufacturer's name? The ever present mind-set is this – I want the "brand name" – don't give me the "generic" product.

These are applicable to our physical possessions, but what about our bodies? (Whose brand are we? Who is our maker? Who created us?) What is the cost and what about the care of our bodies?

We find Paul in chapter six of First Corinthians, starting with verse nine, talking about the sanctity of the body and the fact that the body is holy because it is washed and justified, and because it is the Lord's.

Paul asks a question in verse nineteen – *"What? Know ye not that your body is the temple of the Holy Spirit, Who is in you, whom ye have of God, and ye are not your own?"*

From this verse in scripture I would lift a few words which say very simply – *"Know ye not that your body is the temple of the Holy Spirit?"* This is the question that I would ask us today. I would that our answer to that penetrating question is an empathic yes! Further, I exhort and implore you with these words, "Don't desecrate the temple." "Don't desecrate the temple."

To desecrate means to violate the sanctity of, to profane, to treat irreverently or contemptuously, often in a way that provokes outrage on the part of others (Webster). Now a temple – the physical place of worship, the sanctuary – the Naos (Gk), if you please, is an edifice for religious exercises (II Cor 3:16). In I Cor 6:19 Paul speaks of the physical body of the Christian.

This passage of scripture has great implications for those of us African Americans who are being devastated by a plethora of diseases and afflictions, somatic and psychosomatic that run recklessly rampant through the African American community, like a mighty cyclone, a heart-stopping tornado and a thousand Andrews that nobody controls but the Holy Spirit Who dwells in your body called the temple.

Let us look at this bodily temple from three aspects – **its Creation – its Cost – and its Care.**

The Creation of the Temple

"And God said, let us make Humankind in our image, after our likeness." Genesis 1:26

"So God created Humankind in his own image, in the image of God created He (him); male and female created He them." Genesis 1:27

"And the Lord God formed Humankind of the dust of the ground and breathed into his nostrils the breath of life; and Humankind became a living soul." Genesis 2:7

Ever since that happened from the commencement of time, man's or woman's body has, is and always will be a temple of the Holy Spirit. The Christian's body is a temple possessed by the Holy Spirit, and therefore it belongs to God. Paul's expression of this emphasizes that Christians are God's property, His precious possession, His people whom He has united to Himself in a New Covenant that was effectively sealed by the sacrifice of His Son on Calvary. We're God's workmanship.

A Christian can be considered a Priest in the temple of his/her own body, in which sanctuary he/she serves God and keeps out whatever defiles it.

Which brand are we? We are God's brand. So you live on the mountain top – in your regal splendor – So you live in the valley in your simple bungalow – The deeper question arises – Where and in what do you truly live? You live in your body – temple of the Holy Spirit – God's creation, created by God in the image of God. Guard your physical body like you guard your physical home.

We put electronic alarm systems in our homes for protection and security. Do we protect and secure our bodies? Our bodies – so marvelously put together by God – all 206 bones, to give us support – muscles, tendons, ligaments to render more support – nerves to serve as our own Internet and Websites for our bodies – blood to carry oxygen and nourishment to every cell in our bodies – all sixty trillion of them!

God thinks our bodies are so wonderful that He names His attributes after different parts of them. His omniscience – it is God's eye. His omnipresence – it is God's ear. His omnipotence – it is God's arm.

Man with all of his technological, medical advances has not been able to make a man/woman – Humankind – only God can do that – *"for by Him all things consist."* (Col. 1:17)

Yes, jewelry by Tiffany, suits by Brioni, dresses by Oscar de LaRenta and Liz Claiborne; but your body, the temple of the Holy Spirit is by God!

I say to you that since God has created you, be mindful not to destroy your body. When you destroy your body you destroy God's temple. Though we are established as God's own – man's/woman's inhumanity to man/woman tears at the very fabric of God's creations. The majestic elements of the midnight-heavenly elements manifest the work of God's fingers. His innate power to give and sustain life epitomizes the breath of Almighty God. The sovereign power of God holds true to the fact that the government shall be on His shoulder.

I say to you that you must know and not forget that your bodies are the temples of the Holy Spirit. You must know that your bodies are the only ones which you will ever have in this life. The body must be held in high esteem and cherished to the glory of God.

The temple may become old and its skin wrinkled, its eyes sunken, its shoulders stooped, its legs bowed and its voice weak, but the temple still belongs to God. The Bible declares that *"the earth is the Lord's and the fullness thereof and they the dwell therein."*

Your body, the temple of the Holy Spirit, belongs to God – now, henceforth and forevermore.

There exists no consecrated edifice so sacred as that of the body of the Christian. The beautiful and ageless temple at Jerusalem has been in ruins for centuries. Your body – a living organism of flesh and blood, is the only temple God has here today. That is the frame of flesh in each believer.

We were created by God and for God. The ultimate end of creation is to glorify God. Everything and everyone – on earth – in earth – beneath earth – and above earth are here to beautify, magnify and glorify God.

The Cost of the Body

Not only does the "temple, the body of the Holy Spirit" has a creation, but it also has a cost. We count the cost in everything we purchase – whether it's consciously or subconsciously. There is that lingering question, what does it cost me? What payment plan, revolving charge, do I use here e.g. 30-90 day – no interest? Which amortization schedule do I agree to? E.g. thirty years with a five year balloon payment? When we walk into an automobile showroom looking for that little four wheel chariot of our dreams – check the price and immediately become overcome with "sticker shock" – once we recover then the monthly payments, interest rate and length of contract – 36, 48, or 60 months become an integral part of our budgets. You see everything is bought with a price!

Our bodies – "temples of the Holy Spirit" come with one price – the blood of Jesus who paid it all for you and me. "I know it was the blood, I know it was the blood – one day when I was lost Jesus died upon the cross – I know it was the blood saved me." There on the cross of Calvary our Lord and Master effectively sealed the purchase by the sacrifice on Calvary's rugged brow. Yes, Jesus did pay it all. The beauty in all of this is that everything has been done for you and me – we don't have to shop around looking for a bargain. There is only one brand, called Christian, living in one body called human, interest free. Everything is paid in full by God's son – Jesus Christ.

The writer of "Invictus" wrote "Out of the night that covers me black as a pit from pole to pole, I thank whatever Gods may be for my unconquerable soul. I am the master of my fate, I am the captain of my soul." That was in Invictus, but the book (Bible) says that *"Ye are not your own; for ye are brought with a price."* I Corinthians 6:19-20

The ultimate price was paid by Jesus Christ. The price has been paid fully. I have seen lands, reportedly owned by wealthy men, but all of those lands had heavy mortgages upon them. There is no mortgage on the saints. *"It is finished,"* said Jesus and finished it was.

The body, temple of the Holy Spirit, is worth about $50.00 (fifty dollars) – that is the chemicals, blood vessels, bones, etc. yet we still belong to God.

Man/woman cannot make another man/woman, he/she cannot breathe into his/her nostrils the breath of life and watch man/woman become a living soul. Only God can do that. "It was He who has made us and not we ourselves."

The body, temple of the Holy Spirit, is priceless – a life was given for us out yonder on the hill of shame.

When we think of our bodies, we must count the costs. Our thinking of this would help us to focus on the priceless nature of our being.

Don't ever forget that our purchase price has been paid once and for all and all for once. There aren't any foreclosure procedures applicable to us. No past due notices and late payment charges for us to worry about. We have life-long paid in full mortgages – no monthly payment coupons to worry about – no amortization schedules to contend with in this life. Are you living to the Glory of God in this debt free body purchased by God Himself, owned by God and controlled by God?

The Care of the Temple

Now that we are cognizant of the creation and cost of the temple – the body of the Holy Spirit, what about the care of our temple? Let us examine this last and most important aspect of the temple.

On any given day as we traverse the roadways in our automobiles, we find them inundated with warning signs of every description imaginable. We see – Caution, slippery when wet – Slow, met at work – Resume safe speed – Quiet, hospital zone – Caution, children at play – Speed limit, 50 miles per hour – Dangerous curve, proceed at your own risk – Four way stop – Dangerous intersection, proceed at your own risk, and the list goes on and on. These road signs are there for us to read and obey. There are those of us who may willfully ignore the road signs and travel at our own risk. Sometimes we may get away without a mishap in traveling at our own risk. Yet, sooner or later, we will reap the consequences of our ill-advised disregard for highly visible road signs. Such is the case when you do not exercise due caution in the care of your body, the temple of the Holy Spirit. It goes without saying that your body, created by God and purchased with the blood of Jesus, its cost, must be respected and cared for totally, including your health. Do we care more about our beautiful stained-glass cathedrals of worship than we care about our human bodies, the "living organisms" – who worship in them? Should we do more to remodel, expand and beautify them than we do our bodies? You hold the answers to these provocative, penetrating and unanswered questions.

Relative to health and our bodies, "the temple of the Holy Spirit," I can say to you, empathically, that there are many diseases which plague our bodies.

It is well known that there are many health problems that affect the African American community, uniquely disproportionately.

It goes without saying that the multiplicity of diseases in the African American community emanate from diverse bases of socioeconomic, cultural, ethnic and educational problems.

Late stage diagnosis negates, in most cases, the effectively positive and curative treatment modalities inherent in early diagnosis.

Preventive medicine, effective health education and promotion leading to prevention and early detection comprise essential elements of a sound health education program to help diminish the present trend of crippling diseases that plague our communities.

In our bloated billion dollar health care budget less than one percent is spent on prevention. This is astounding!

In one recent edition of the American Cancer Society's booklet on Cancer Facts and Figures for African Americans, some startling facts are presented. Let us see what is said about your body, the temple of the Holy Spirit. Studies on A Profile of the African American Population have shown the following –

Population:

African Americans are among the largest minority groups in the United States. The majority of African Americans in the United States are descendants of slaves from Africa.

Family Structure:

The proportion of married-couple families in the African American population has declined over the past two decades. The proportion of African American families maintained by a single parent has increased.

Education:

African Americans have made significant gains in education.

Occupation:

A few years ago, African American males had a higher labor force participation rate than females, however, a smaller proportion of men than women held managerial or professional positions. Men were most likely employed as operators, fabricators, or laborers, while women were most likely to work in technical, sales and administrative support.

Income:

In the recent past, income was strongly related to family structure, ranging from $12,500 for families with no husband present to $35,540 for married-couple families. More black families had incomes below poverty level.

Health Status:

Disparities in socioeconomic status between Whites and African Americans have resulted in disparities in access, availability and utilization of health care services. In particular, African Americans have poorer insurance coverage and poorer access to high quality primary care than their White counterparts.

African Americans are 62% more likely to use emergency departments for ambulatory care than Whites (55 vs. 34 visits per 100 persons). In contrast, the use of physician's offices was 16%

lower for African Americans than for Whites.

Studies have shown an association between social status and knowledge, attitudes and behaviors regarding health matters. Individuals with low income are generally less knowledgeable about disease and health status, are often hard to recruit for screening and other health service programs, and often delay seeking medical care.

African Americans have the highest (age-adjusted) total death rate of any race or ethnic group in the United States. In particular, rates are very high relative to the total U.S. population of AIDS, infant mortality and homicide.

Chronic disease is also a problem for African Americans. Heart disease, cancer and cerebrovascular diseases are the three leading causes of death in this population. In 1992 these diseases killed 5 times more African Americans than AIDS, homicide and diseases of infancy combined.

The foregone information relative to studies done was for you to get a better picture of our African American brothers'/sisters' plight in our communities.

I can see malignant hypertension (high blood pressure), untreated sugar diabetes, crippling arthritis, cancers in all parts of this temple. Prostate cancers in African American males cause us to die younger and in greater proportions than Whites. In addition, lung cancers, color and breast cancers, AIDS and chronic cigarette smoking are helping to devastate our community. These are in addition to the violence – gunshot wounds, stabbings and knife wounds, many of which are inflicted teenagers and those younger.

Listen, listen! 100,000 children take guns to school daily. 160,000 children miss school daily because of the fear of guns. 40 children are killed or injured by firearms in schools on a daily basis (figures from the Criminal Justice Institute). **Violence to the body must stop!**

Heart disease kills 700,000 each year in this country. If we would control our blood pressure, exercise and stay off of fatty foods, we could begin to reduce these devastating deaths.

There are those of us who smoke "religiously" on a daily basis. Tobacco kills 435,000 people per year, let alone the associated lung diseases related to smoking – bronchitis and emphysema.

Chronic alcoholism, drinking liquor, kills another 120,000 people per year. So you can see that tobacco and alcohol kill 555,000 people per year.

There are some diseases that we African Americans inherit, e.g. Sickle Cell Anemia. We have no control over that because we couldn't choose our parents. Yet there are many other maladies which we inflict upon ourselves, e.g. sexually transmitted diseases and hepatitis among others. Just as there is a disproportionate amount of social ills, socioeconomic problems, poverty, ignorance, lack of education and substandard housing, there also is a greater number of mortalities from the cradle to the grave in the African American community.

Are you helping to stave off this ruthless onslaught on the temple of the Holy Spirit? I ask – What are you doing? We are all in this fight (battle) together, because in the words of John Donne, *"No man/woman is an island entire of itself. We are all a piece of the continent, a part of the main."*

Are you destroying your "temple?"

Have you not seen violent destruction of human life and limb – no one is truly safe.

My brother, you may have a normal PSA test for prostate cancer, cholesterol, ideal weight, normal chest x-ray, normal stress test and you exercise 5x a week, not only that but you don't smoke, drink, use drugs and abuse your body. Yet, if you are African American, your chances of getting killed are 1 in 27, whereas the chances of a White male getting killed are 1 in 205.

My sister, you may be in the best state of health – e.g. you have a normal mammogram, pap smear, blood pressure, cholesterol, and you too may exercise 5x a week, complemented with the daily flossing of your teeth – yet, in this society, you are not immune to violent acts of crime – e.g. drive-by-shootings and home invasions.

The young, pregnant teenager or adult who seeks no prenatal care, and subsequently has a low birth-weight baby gives us –

society – a costly, usually preventable problem. That is one which costs approximately $10,000, as opposed to approximately $1,500 under normal circumstances.

Medical science has advanced to the point when many experiments are being done on your body, the temple of the Holy Spirit, e.g. cloning, partial birth abortions, physician assisted suicide. Medical ethics have not kept pace with the technological advances in medicine. We ask the question – What's next?

I am sure that you have seen deaths that you know possibly could have been prevented.

Let us not forget that the African American church stands as an immovable landmark in the community. The church is pivotal as a place of refuge for our multi-faceted problems.

You must strive to add life to your years rather than years to your life.

What is life?

Shakespeare said in Macbeth:
"Life is but a walking shadow, a poor player that struts and frets his hour upon the stage and is heard no more. It is a tale told by an idiot full of sound and fury signifying nothing."

Paul Lawrence Dunbar, in his poem "Life," said these words –
"From a crust of bread and a corner to sleep in – A minute to smile and an hour to weep in – from a pint of joy to a peck of trouble. And never a laugh, but the moans come double – That's life."

Jesus of Nazareth said, *"I am the way, the truth and the life. No man cometh to the Father but by me."* No White man, no Black man, no educated man.

I respectfully exhort each of you here today to become a committee of one in taking charge of your health – from this moment on. That's the starting point.

Become a sterling example for your families and churches – get regular medical checkups, exercise and follow a proper diet low in fat and salt.

You are critical in the process of healthy bodies and **Preventive Health Education**.

In 1976, President Gerald Ford's wife had breast cancer. A patient of mine saw it on television and felt a lump in her breast.

I diagnosed the breast cancer and performed a mastectomy on her. She came for help in time. Why do I say that? Because she lived through open-heart surgery, hypertension, arthritis and diabetes.

> *"Know ye not that your body is the temple of the Holy Spirit who is you, whom ye have God, and ye are not your own?"*
> I Corinthians 6:19

Your body is the Creation of God. The COST was paid in full by His Son, Jesus Christ and the Care has been entrusted to you.

That body of yours may be weak and weather beaten from years of hard work in the vineyard.

Care for it – don't desecrate the temple!

Your body may need to be propped up on every leaning side, but it's still the temple of the Holy Spirit.

Care for it – don't desecrate the temple!

You may have been given the ultimate diagnosis based on bodily afflictions, just don't desecrate the temple because ye are washed – washed in the blood of the lamb.

SERMON TWO
Is There a Doctor in the House?

> *And a woman having an issue of blood twelve years, who had spent all her living upon physicians, neither could be healed by any..."*
> Luke 8:43

> *."..came behind Him, and touched the border of His garment; and immediately her issue of blood stanched or stopped."*
> Luke 8:44

On October 3, 1976, a bright, sunny Sunday morning in South Florida, my father, a preacher for 56 years, suffered a stroke, while preaching. The condition worsened on Monday morning, and he was taken to the hospital. His condition rapidly deteriorated into paralysis and speechlessness. He was in a coma.

My mother and sister began calling me to come, quickly, to see him. My mother continually said that she knew he would get better and recover if I were there. I went to see him in the hospital. His state was one of semi-consciousness with labored respirations and nearly imperceptible speech. I leaned over his bed, touched him, and asked him how he felt. His answer to me was that "I want to get well." Five days later, he died. Yes, he died. Despite my response to my mother's call, my presence at his bedside, concluding with my touching of his hand – I could not improve his condition. I touched him but I was powerless to save him – he still died. I loved him but I couldn't save him. For a while I felt responsible and guilty for his death. My mother continued to assure me that there wasn't anything that I could do. She reminded me that it was the Lord's will.

I dealt with him on a human level and realized that only the supernatural divine healing power of Jesus Christ could have made any difference in his outcome.

Some of you may be able to relate to similar stories in your lives or those of your family or friends. The final result in the end of illness is quite often death.

In St. Luke 8:43 we find these words –
"And a woman having an issue of blood twelve years, who had spent all of her living upon physicians, neither could be healed by any." "Came behind him and touched the border (or hem) of His garment; and immediately her issue of blood stopped."
Luke 8:43-44

From these familiar verses I pose a question to you and to me.

Is There a Doctor in the House?

When I thought of a true healing physician, my mind traversed the country to the many elite and famous hospitals, prominent medical centers and renowned medical schools. My thoughts went to the Mayo Clinic, with its state-of-the-art medical facilities – but I couldn't find the physician there either. I went to Meharry Medical College, Harvard, Johns Hopkins, Stanford, and Howard Universities; these institutions were void of the premiere doctor that I so desperately and diligently sought.

The great heart, liver and lung transplant centers did not hold the answer to my search. Super-specialists from across the country were weighed in the balance and found wanting. They were called in consultation. Yet, they couldn't answer my call.

Finally, I consulted Doctor Luke, "the beloved physician" who wrote about the woman with an issue of blood for twelve years. She was miraculously healed by Jesus Christ – the great physician. In the pericope of the woman with an issue of blood, Jesus is the healer's healer and the physician's physician. The Bible is replete with events of Jesus' healing, of the body, mind and spirit. The healing was consummated immediately. There wasn't any need to wait for relief.

As in life itself, Jesus, who is life, sets the place in the ministry of healing. He never carried an otoscope and audiometer to measure hearing. Yet He restored hearing to the deaf. You do remember Mark telling you:

> *"when he came unto the Sea of Galilee – through the midst of the coasts of Decapolis – they brought unto Him one that was deaf – He put his fingers in his ears and straightaway his ears were opened."*
> Mark 7:31, 33, 35

He never carried an opthalmoscope for eye examinations. There weren't any eye charts. Yet He restored sight to the blind. Go ask Mark. Don't you remember when He went out of Jericho and He met old blind Bartimaeus, son of Timaeus, sitting by the highway begging. Jesus stopped – asked Bartimaeus – What wilt thou that I should do unto thee? – Bartimaeus answered, *"That I might receive my sight."* – Jesus said, *"Go thy way, thy faith has made thee well,"* – and immediately he received his sight. (Mark 10:46-52).

He never received a degree in Speech Therapy. Yet he removed a speech impediment and loosed a stammering tongue.

Don't you remember when He was on the sea of Galilee and called out, "Be opened" and straightaway the string of the tongue of one with a speech impediment was loosed. Mk 7:31-37.

He didn't take a residency in orthopedic surgery, neither was he a chiropractor. He never manipulated withered limbs. Yet He restored the power to walk in those who were lame. If you don't believe me – go down to the pool of Bethesda and see how the man (humankind) who had not walked for 38 years did indeed walk when Jesus told him to *"Rise – take up thy bed and walk."* Jn 5:8

Jesus didn't even take a residency in psychiatry. Yet He opened His office for psychiatric consultation and treatment in the middle of the graveyard, at night, in the country of Gerasenes. You do remember when He, Jesus, the great physician, broke the bonds of that certain man and drove the demons out of him into the wilderness.

He never performed CPR (cardio pulmonary resuscitation). Yet He restored life to those who were dead in body, mind and spirit. Before Jesus got to Jairus' house, his daughter had died. Everybody started crying. Jesus said, *"Weep not; she is not dead, but sleepeth."* Luke 8:50.

They laughed him to scorn – He put all of them out of the house – took Jairus' daughter by the hand and called, *"Maid, arise."* (Lk 8:54) – and she arose straightaway, immediately.

We find Jesus on His way to heal Jairus' twelve year old daughter who was near death. As Jesus traversed the terrain towards Jairus' house, many people surrounded or thronged him.

St. Luke, the beloved physician, tells us *"and a woman having an issue of blood twelve years who had spent all her living upon physicians, neither could be healed by any."* (Luke 8:43)

Mark said *"She was no better but rather grew worse."* (Mark 5:26)

This woman started bleeding when Jairus' daughter was born.

She was very sick, weak and pale from twelve years of blood loss. She was extremely anemic. Her life was being drained from her body.

Twelve years is a mighty long time to be constantly bleeding – losing blood without its replenishment by blood transfusions or iron tablet therapy replacement. She was weak, she continued to work and pay doctors who took her 'living' and couldn't help her. She only went to the Master when she was broke and destitute. There weren't any social service agencies or welfare programs available to her. She was there, as a suspended puppet, dangling between a heaven of hope and an earth of hopelessness.

Long before man understood all of the blood elements he knew that it was the source of life. I can hear them singing, *"I know it was the blood I know it was the blood saved me. One day when I was lost Jesus died upon the cross."* The book of Leviticus declares that the life of flesh is in the blood. (Lev. 17:11)

Blood is mentioned more than 500 times in the Bible; it became a promise of atonement to believers. The shedding of Christ's blood on Calvary represents the hope of atonement.

Blood does for humankind what the mighty oceans do for the smallest forms of life. In performing its essential functions, it moves swiftly and powerfully.

Blood is composed of a society of diverse, solid cells, each with specific duties and coexisting in critical proportions. Should the population of only one element fail, life would be threatened. You can readily see that the life of this woman with the issue of blood, was at risk.

The list of blood's daily chores is astonishing. It supplies the vital gas, oxygen, to each of the other sixty trillion cells in the body. It transports food, wastes and hormonal messengers. It rushes to the stomach after meals, to the lungs during exertion, and to the face in embarrassment. It cools where there is overheating, and warms where there is eminent danger of freezing. It defends the body, destroying foreign invaders. If the walls of a blood vessel burst, blood itself quickly seals and mends the vessel so that massive bacterial invasion does not take place. In short, blood is the river enriching the continent called humankind.

Now the red blood cell is an untiring and faithful servant. Unperturbed by disease or infection, it will dissipate itself completely with work – it makes 75,000 trips between the lungs and the body's tissues – in just four short months. Blood attends to life's fires – ceaselessly traversing through the body, and the cells, it faithfully tends the life of life. Life emanates from power produced by cells.

Blood has been called a fabric which heals itself. Unlike any other fabric devised by humankind, blood will close torn tissue, magically producing its own threads to weave the tear together again. Being guided by invisible hands with invisible needles, fine fibers are woven into being at the site of injury, sealing off the blood, preventing its escape. After completing its work the fabric, likened to the cloak of a magician, is lifted to demonstrate the efficacy of its labors.

Despite the beneficial effects of blood in sustaining life, by Levitical standards, this woman was unclean. Leviticus 15:19 – And if a woman have an issue and her issue in her flesh be blood, she shall be put apart seven days; and whosoever toucheth her shall be unclean until the evening.

> "And everything that she lieth upon in her separation shall be unclean; everything also that she sitteth upon shall be unclean." (Lev. 15:20)

By these Levitical laws, she was basically unclean and an outcast. I stand here to tell you today that the Bible declares that *"Blotting out the handwriting of ordinances that was against us, which was contrary to us, and took it out of the way, nailing it to His cross."* (Col. 2:14). You see this Levitical law was nailed to the cross with Jesus.

I have seen women bleed thirty days or more, but I have never seen one bleed for twelve years in my 35 years of practice. That's a long time to suffer.

After having become broke and destitute, she heard of Jesus, came in the crowd behind, and touched His garment.

She had heard of Jesus – something divine and spiritual

happened to her because *"faith cometh by hearing and hearing by the word of God."* (Rom. 10:17). She walked by faith and not by sight (II Cor. 5:7).

That woman was a nobody until she met Jesus. I can hear her ask the question – Is there a doctor in the house?"

She was lost in the maze of a chronic, unremitting, unrelenting condition – bleeding daily for twelve years. Yes, twelve years of weakness, pain, loss of appetite and weight from poor nutrition – add to that dizziness, a rapid heart rate, a clouded sensorium (mentality), and you have a treacherous state of medical affairs. She was down and out – there are people around her, but she was still lost! Her state of lostness was incomprehensibly devastating to this solitary figure – up against the odds of an apparent, uncaring world. She heard of Jesus who was passing by to heal someone else – Yes, Jesus, the one whose Father created those physicians who were unable to help her – except to take her money – her "living" – and not be able to render any help – not only did they not help her, but they made her worse. It appears as though she was down on her knees, crawling to touch the hem of His garment.

That lost woman, that nobody, thought, "If I can touch His garment, I shall be whole." Her touching Him was earnest. It was a touch of faith.

There are multitudes who superficially touch Jesus with their spurious respect. No doubt is left that the religion of Christ is respected. Christianity is a most respectable institution. Through it all this respect is not like that touch which she gave in the earnest purpose of faith and need.

Some touch Jesus with their opinions. Those opinions, with their shaky intellectual authenticity, give them no sincere connection with the Savior.

The essential thing is not what we think about Him, but what He Himself, in His personal relations, and His healing, life-giving power is to us.

Others touch Jesus through sacraments and ceremonies. The idea of the woman appears to have been of this kind. She thought, "If I may touch His garment, I shall be whole;" whereas we know that the virtue of strength went out of Him.

Another group may choose to touch Jesus timidly. They commune Him occasionally with pathetic impulses of inconsistent fanaticism during seasons of inspiration: Easter, Christmas, or they keep it a secret of which they are ashamed. We must, indeed, respect the modesty of sincere faith, exemplified by this woman with an issue of blood.

Not only that, but there are other various touches. There is the unbeliever's "touch," like the disrespectful touch of the profane hands of the soldiers who nailed Jesus to the cross of Calvary.

There are countless thousands who handle Jesus' Person; they refuse to leave Him alone; yet as they "touch" Him they only "touch" Him bringing judgment and unending death, dealing condemnation upon their own souls, because their "touch" is one of unbelief.

The cold "touch" of the critic is forever present. He/she is not profane, he/she is not irreverent, he/she is simply critical. The object of their folly is an assault on the character of Jesus, during their fallacious test. More commonly, there is the fashionable "touch." These are they who are prevalent in all our churches and worship centers, most likely once a week; they have their false expression of praise, their tribute to pay, and they pay it because society expects that from them.

Finally, there is one in which a greater number of persons seem to "touch" Him without receiving any assistance whatsoever because it is the "touch" of indifference.

These are some of the different ways we may "touch" Christ and yet get no healing benefit. We should ask ourselves, How are we to "touch" Christ with good effect?

2. Joseph S. Excell, The Biblical Illustrator, St. Luke, Chapter VIII (Grand Rapids, Michigan, Baker Book House 1966.78).

There may be many difficulties as that poor woman, e.g. no blood, no money, no property, no friends; she was LOST – her state of Lost-ness was unbearable. The very nature of her disease was one which made her shrink back from anything like publicity. She might have waited until He was not surrounded by a crowd – waited for a more favorable opportunity. She says to herself, "I am going to be healed." She does not say, "I am going to try."

Look at the patient that nobody. Now she might have put many physicians together, and their many failures have rationally inferred that her case was beyond hope.

Is there a doctor in the house? Look at her again – her courage. She was a woman who had suffered from a very grievous sickness, which had drained away her life. Yes, she was bleeding in body, mind and spirit.

Is there a doctor in the house? Her constitution had been sapped and undermined, and her very existence had become one of constant suffering and weakness and yet what courage and spirit she displayed. She was ready to go through fire and through water to obtain health. She would not resign herself to the inevitable until she had used every effort to preserve life and regain health. This woman's marvelous hopefulness is to be admired. She still believes that she can be cured. She could not forget that the disease itself was incurable and that she had endured frequent disappointments. Yet she was not dismayed: her faith rose superior to her bitter experience and she believed in the Lord.

Another difficulty was there – she had no money. Another difficulty was her extreme sickness at that time. Is there a doctor in the house?

Longing

Her state of lost-ness was abated because she heard of Jesus – went and found Him in a crowd. This helped to satisfy her longing for relief of years filled with hopelessness and despair. This is a sad, sad case! We are told that she had suffered many things of many physicians. Human physicians could not heal. More suffering was her only reward for trusting and spending. She had only suffered – not healed nor relieved. She grew worse. She was a woman who had spent all that she had only to suffer more from her disease; in her despair, would go to One who at least demanded no fee, and who was reported to have wrought many marvelous cures. But why does she select the hem or border of His garment?

Perhaps because she thought herself unworthy to do more. Perhaps because in her faith she thought even that would be enough. Perhaps simply because she thought the border of His garment might be most easily touched without attracting attention.

According to the Hebrew law she was impure, and made all she touched impure; but she ventured to touch Jesus, and, instead of making Him unclean, He made her clean and whole.

Who then, is the feeble woman that struggles through the swaying crowd, and watches her opportunity to stoop and lay her hand on the Healer's garment. This is a poor woman, a nobody affected for twelve years with a disorder, a hemorrhage, which rendered her "unclean" in the eyes of the law so that she could neither enter temple nor synagogue. Your disorder may be high blood pressure, sugar diabetes, incurable cancer, or crippling arthritis. In some cases similar situations prevail today, e.g. HIV Aids victims who are shunned and cast out, not only that but addicts and prostitutes. We must reach out and embrace those who are down and out – "the least of these."

This woman had a longing for life. She used the likeliest means she could think of. She went to physicians. Now, physicians are men or women set apart on purpose to deal with human illnesses. No doubt she met with some who boasted that they could heal her complaint at once. They began saying, "You have tried old so-and-so, but he is a mere quack; mine is a scientific remedy. Come with me." Many pretenders to new revelations are abroad, but they are physicians of no value.

Many·thronged and pressed upon Christ; many touched His clothes. Yet only one touched Him. Why did this touch attract the particular attention of the Savior? It was the touch of a sufferer whose case, before that touch, had been desperate. It was the touch of faith. A touch of somebody. She didn't call 911. She had 911 in her hand and heart. She was in the office of Jesus Christ – the true emergency physician.

Why did the Savior ask the question, "Who touched me?" This excited the wonder of the disciples. Not from ignorance. Not from exhaustion. Not from displeasure. But to show that He makes the difference between thronging and touching Him. Virtue or strength went out of Him – and she was healed immediately, and in a miraculous way.

She didn't make an appointment to see Jesus. Notice that this woman was not sent to the lab to get a CBC (blood count), chest x-ray, EKG and other tests and from there to the internist or hematologist to be cleared medically for surgery. There wasn't any need to call surgery scheduling for operating room time. Don't call the lab! Don't call the internist! Don't call the hematologist! Don't alert surgery! Jesus Christ is in town. **Yes there is a doctor in the house.** I say Jesus Christ is here. He has the lab, internist, surgeon, pharmacy and the operating room locked up in the hem of His garment. The healing was complete. The bleeding stopped immediately! It was her faith that bridged the gap from hopelessness to health. You see when Dr. Hamilton does a D & C operation to stop bleeding from the womb (uterus) or even a hysterectomy to stop hemorrhage, he must give blood transfusions.

Jesus said, "Daughter, be of good comfort; thy faith hath made thee well. Go in peace." (Lk 8:48). No need to come back to my office – no prescriptions to be filled – no packing to be removed – by the way, there's no need to even check your blood count – you have all of your blood – all 5-1/2 pints. I can hear Him say, "daughter, your transfusion started on Mt. Calvary's rugged brow when they cut Me and I bled and died for you. Why? Because there is a fountain filled with blood drawn from Immanuel's veins. Sinners plunge beneath that flood – lose all their guilty stains.

Jesus, who is the doctor in the house, is strong. **He's** so strong that somebody had called **Him** a fortress that you can hide behind when your enemies are pursuing you – Somebody else has called **Him** a leaning post. Abraham leaned on **Him**. Isaac leaned on **Him**. Jacob leaned on **Him**. Christians all over the world are leaning on **Him** today. Christians right here are leaning on **Him** today.

Yes, there is a doctor in the house, and His name is Jesus.

Glossary

By-product - That which comes as a result of an entity's normal evolution.

Christian Health Lecture Series - Lectures conducted at the local church on various pertinent health topics and issues.

Community Health Fair - One that involves the entire community with the participation of several churches and the local Health Department in Community Health Outreach.

Church Health Ministry Linkages - Those linked with local health care agencies, e.g. local Health Department.

Health - Simply, this is the absence of disease.

Health Academy - Comprised of youth (ages five years through high school) where they are taught at an early age about health and healthy lifestyles.

Health Consciousness - That state of one's thinking or awareness relative to his/her health.

Health Disciples - Members of the Health Academy.

Holistic - Related to the total view of health, e.g. : The body, mind and spirit.

Importunate Diseases - Those diseases which are bothersome and persistent.

Inter-faith (denominational) Health Partnerships - Those existing between churches of different faiths.

Medical Compliance - For the betterment of all, to follow the doctors orders.

Minister of Health and Wellness - The Medical Director who is charged with the administration and teaching in the ministry.

Periodic Health Screenings - Those done to detect disease states at an early stage, e.g. PSA blood test for prostate cancer.

Speakers Bureau - List of former, present and future health lecture speakers.

Warning Signs - Those signs, e.g. blood in stool, etc., that will alert the person to a serious problem.

Wellness - The state of being sound and healthy.

Bibliography

American Medical News, February 6, 1995.

Bakken, Kenneth, The Call to Wholeness: Health and Spiritual Journey, New York, Crosswords, 1990.

Barnes, Freddie I., Consumer and Health Education in the African American Church, 1993. Bearon, L.B., Koenig, H.G., Religious Cognitions and Use of Prayer in Health and Illness, Gerontologist, 30(2): 249-53, 1990 Apr.

Benson, Herbert, M.D., Timeless Healing, First Fireside Edition, Simon and Schuster, 1997

Birch S. Chambers S., Canadian Medical Association Journal, 149(5): 607-12, 1993 Sep 1. To Each According to Need: A Community-based Approach to Allocating Health Care Resources.

Brown, Dr. Gary LE, ed., Religious Involvement and Health Status Among African American Males, Journal of the National Medical Association, 86(11): 825-31, 1994.

Carter, James Calvin, Preaching About Health and Wellness in the Black Church, 1991.

Coke, M, Correlates of Life Satisfaction Among Elderly African Americans, Journal of Gerontology 47(5): P316-20, 1992 Sep.

Conroy, Mary Carol, ed., The Historical Development of the Health Care Ministry of the Sisters of Charity of Leavenworth, Kansas, Volume 45-08-A of Dissertation Abstracts International, Page 2417.

Daaleman TP, Dease, DE Jr., Patient Attitudes Regarding Physician Inquiry Into Spiritual and Religious Issues, Journal of Family Practice, 39(6): 564-8, 1994 Dec.

Davis, DT, Bustamonte A., Brown CP, Wolde-Badik G., Savage, EW Chereg X., Howland L. The Urban Church and Cancer Control: A Source of Social Influence in Minority Communities Public Health Reports. 109(4): 500-6, 1994 Jan.-Aug.

Erwin DO, Spatz TS, Turturro CL, Development of an African-American Role Model Intervention to Increase Breast Self-Examination and Mammography. Journal of Cancer Education 7(4) 311-9, 1992 Winter.

Grodin, M.A., Religious Advance Directives: The Convergence of Law, Religion, Medicine and Public Health, American Journal of Public Health 83(6): 899-903, 1993 Jun.

Hamilton, Edwin Harvey, "The Health and Wellness Ministry in the African American Church: Preventive Health Education." Diss., United Theological Seminary, 1997

James, Philip Karl, The Education and Management of the Distribution of Preventive Health Care: The Role of The Church and Inner City Head Start Parents, 1993.

Johnson, Leath Columbus, Jr., ed, The Development and Implementation of a Health Ministry for the First Baptist Church, Statesville, North Carolina, Volume 54/03-B of Dissertation Abstracts International, Page 1324. 448 Pages Drew University, 1992, D.Min.

Jones, A. W., A Survey of General Practitioners' Attitudes to the Involvement of Clergy in Patient Care, British Journal of Geneva Practice, 40(336): 280-3, 1990 Jul.

Kamanyika SK, Charleston JB, Lose Weight and Win: A Church-based Weight Loss Program for Blood Pressure Control Among Black Women, Patient Education and Counseling 19(1): 19-32, 1992 Feb. Kennerly, Melvin Anthony, A Study of Selected Health and Wellness Programs and Their Usefulness in Impacting the African American Community, 1993.

Koenig, H.G., Bearon, L.B., Dayringer, R., Physician Perspectives on the Role of Religion in the Physician-Older Patient Relationship, Journal of family Practice, 28(4): 441-8, 1989 Apr.

King, D.E., Bushwick, B., Beliefs and Attitudes of Hospital Inpatients About Faith Healing and Prayer, Journal of Family Practice, 39(4): 349-52, 1994 Oct.

King, D.E., Sobal, J., Haggerty, J. 3d, Dent, M., Patton, D., Experiences and Attitudes About Faith Healing Among Family Physicians, Journal of Family Practice, 35(2): 158-62, 1992 Aug.

King James Version of the Bible, The.

Levin, J.S., Religion and Health: Is There an Association, Is it Valid, and Is it Causal?, Social Science and Medicine, 38(11): 1475-82, 1994 Jun.

Levin, J.S.,Vanderpool, H.Y., Is Religion Therapeutically Significant for Hypertension, Social Science and Medicine, 29(1): 69-78, 1989.

Levine, D.M., Becker, D.M., Bone, L.R., Stillman, F.A., Tuggle, M.C., 2d, Prentice, M., Carter, J., Filippeli, J., A Partnership with Minority Populations: A Community Model of Effectiveness Research, Ethnicity and Disease. 2(3): 296-305, 1992 Summer.

Martin, Dale, The Corinthian Body, New Haven, CT, Yale University Press, 1985

McKee, D.D., Chappel, J.N., Spirituality and Medical Practice, Journal of Family Practice 35(2): 201, 205-8, 1992 Aug.

Mermann, A.C., Spiritual Aspects of Death and Dying, Yale Journal of Biology and Medicine, 65(2): 137-42, 1992 Mar-Apr.

Moore, Frank, Health and Wellness in the African American Churches in the Twenty-First Century An On-Going Program, 1990.

Newsome, J., ed., Nurses in the African American Church, ABNF Journal 5(5): 134:7, 1994 Sept.-Oct.

Pilch, John, Wellness Your Invitation to a Full Life, Winston Press, 1981

Proctor, Samuel Dewitt, ed., The Substance of Things Hoped For: A Memoir of African-American Faith, New York, G.P. Putnam°s Sons, 1995.

Reed, P.G., Spirituality and Well-being In Terminally Ill Hospitalized Adults, Research in Nursing and Health, 10(5): 335-44, 1987 Oct.

Reed, P.G., Religiousness Among Terminally Ill and Healthy Adults, Research in Nursing and Health, 9(1): 35-41, 1986 Mar.

Rubin RH, Billingsley A., Caldwell CH, ed., The Role of the Black Church in Working with Black Adolescents, Adolescence, 1994 Summer. Salewski, R.M., Meeting Holistic Health Needs Through a Religious Organization: The Congregation, The Journal of Holistic Nursing. 11(2): 183-96, 1993 Jun.

Schmied LA, Jost KJ, Church Attendance, Religiosity, and Health

Psychological Reports, 74(1): 145-6, 1994 Feb.

Smith ED., Hypertension with Church-Based Education: A Pilot Study, Journal of National Black Nurses Association, 6(1): 19-28, 1992, Fall-Winter.

Stillman FA, Bone LR. Land C. Levine DM. Becker DM., Heart, Body, and Soul: A Church-Based Smoking Cessation Program for Urban African-American Preventive Medicine, 22(3) 335-49, 1993 May.

Thomas SB, Quinn SC. Billingsley A. Caldwell C. The Characteristics of Northern Black Churches with Community Health Outreach Programs, 1994 Apr, American Journal of Public Health 84(4): 575-9.

Zavertnik JJ. Strategies for Reaching Poor Blacks and Hispanics in Dade County, Florida, Cancer 72(3) Suppl: 1088-92, 1993 Aug 1.

Zimmerman MA, Maton KI, Life-Style and Substance Use Among Male African-American Urban Adolescents, A Cluster Analytic Approach, American Journal of Community Psychology, 20(1): 121-38, 1992 Feb.

The Health and Wellness Ministry in the African American Church

**Edwin Harvey Hamilton, M.D., D. Min.
Physician-Theologian-Author**

The Health and Wellness Ministry in the African American Church

**Dr. Hamilton being hooded by mentor
Wyatt Tee Walker, D. Min at graduation**

George Rawls, M.D. receiving proclamation from
Dr. Hamilton at the 2004 Health Care Conference

The Health and Wellness Ministry in the African American Church

Dr. Hamilton presenting proclamation to Surgeon General Joycelyn Elders, M.D.

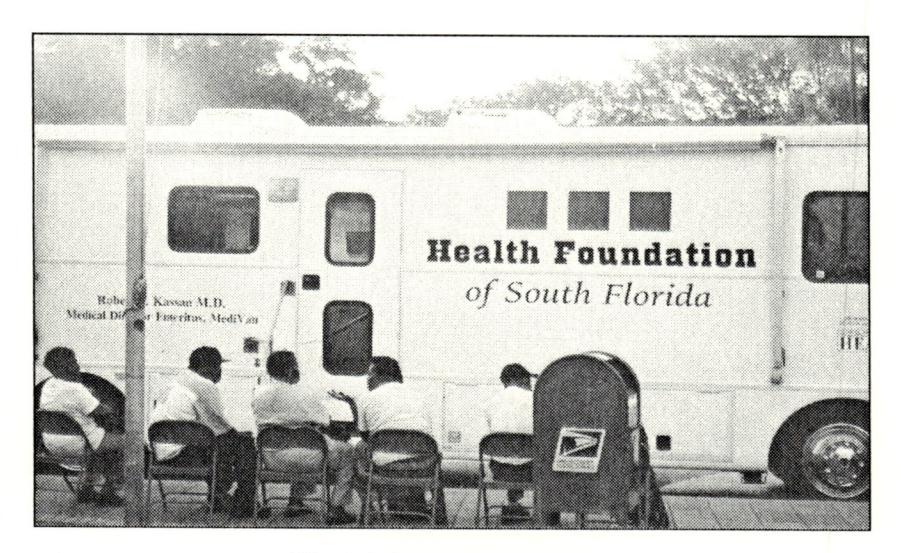

Health Foundation Van

The Health and Wellness Ministry in the African American Church

**Edwin H. Hamilton, M.D., Min.,
standing in front of the van**

The Health and Wellness Ministry in the African American Church

**Dr. Hamilton at the volunteer
evening clinic – Lauderdale Lakes Complex**

The Health and Wellness Ministry in the African American Church

Dr. Hamilton, sitting in the van